Man the Builder

Man the Builder

John Harvey

Fellow of the Society of Antiquaries
and Consultant Architect to Winchester College

PRIORY PRESS LIMITED

Social History of Science Library

Man the Astronomer Patrick Moore
Man the Aviator Charles Harvard Gibbs-
           Smith
Man the Builder John Harvey
Man the Explorer G R Crone
Man the Farmer Robert Trow-Smith
Man the Navigator E W Anderson
Man and the Wheel D S Benson
Man the Industrialist Peter Hobday
Man the Healer W R Trotter
Man the Toolmaker Michael Grey
Man and Measurement Keith Ellis
Man and Money Keith Ellis
Man the Shipbuilder Maurice Griffiths
Man the Steelmaker W K V Gale

SBN 85078 139 6
Copyright © 1973 by John Harvey
First Published in 1973 by
Priory Press Ltd
Text set in Baskerville
and printed in Great Britain
by Page Bros (Norwich) Ltd, Norwich

Contents

List of Illustrations

Foreword

The subject of man as a builder is so vast that a short introduction can touch upon only a small part of it. For that reason this book attempts in its text to give only a connected summary dealing with buildings in Britain, and mainly in England at that. To give a wider background, a date chart has been added, including works from 753 BC (the traditional founding of Rome) to the present day. This chart shows buildings of Britain, of the continent of Europe, and of the East and America. For many countries (notably China and Japan, and ancient Mexico and Peru) there are few entries because either the buildings or the dates are lost. On the other hand, it has been possible to bring together a satisfactory series of dated works for the regions to which we, in Britain, are most indebted for the forms that our buildings have taken.

Change and development proceed at a different pace in different countries. To a great extent they depend upon political conditions and upon economic prosperity. So we shall find, by looking at the chart, that when for example very few buildings were of any importance in Britain (in the Dark Ages), a great deal was happening elsewhere. The cathedral of Santa Sophia at Constantinople (Istanbul) was being designed and

"Building the Tower of Babel" as shown by a Parisian illuminator c. 1433 in the Bedford Missal (British Museum) (*facing page*)

9

built in the middle of a great gap of nearly three hundred years in British architecture. Still in that gap, but even farther away in China, the Great Stone Bridge was build in AD 605–616. It has a span of 123 feet and was designed by a famous builder, Li Chun. In Britain it was well over a thousand years later that a bridge, of just the same kind but even bigger (140 feet) was built at Pontypridd in 1752–1755. This was the third attempt of the mason, William Edwards, who designed it. We do not know if Edwards could somehow have learned of the clever method used so long before in China.

What is known is that in many ways China and the Far East were ahead of Europe. Printing, re-invented in Europe in the fifteenth century, had been known in China for hundreds of years. The Chinese official Board of Works in AD 1091 issued an important handbook on *Methods of Building Construction;* and in 1103 it was printed. Nearer home, buildings with pointed arches were known in the Near East for three or four centuries before they reached Europe at the start of the Gothic style. What eventually became the typically British way of building owed a great deal to Persia, Armenia and Turkey.

At first sight it may seem impossible that, before there were newspapers or regular postal services, still less telegraph, telephone or wireless, ideas should have travelled so far and so fast. The fact is that they did travel, carried by individuals. The carriers might be traders, or artists, or simply ordinary folk who went on a pilgrimage and came back full of what they had seen in Spain or Italy, Egypt and the Holy Land. A very few of the human links were real explorers who went out deliberately to discover what the hidden parts of the world were like. Through all these people, of different nations and religions, came fragments of knowledge and of skill. Building was only one of man's activities to be profoundly affected by all this coming and going, and for that reason the date chart at the end of this book includes mention of some great events and inventions happening at the same time. The great buildings take their place as vital pieces contributing to the story of Man.

A book of this kind owes a great deal to many other books, too many for all to be named. For readers who wish to find out more on this subject, a short list is printed (page 96) of bibliographies of the subject and of titles dealing with aspects of building in England, and with the great buildings of other parts of the world. For help in finding material, especially for the date chart, I am greatly indebted to York City Library and to its Reference Librarian Mr Maurice Smith. Other libraries which have contributed important information are those of the British Museum, the

Pontypridd, Glamorgan: the great arch (140 feet) of 1752–55 (foreground) by William Edwards, who rediscovered the principle of the Chinese Great Stone Bridge, built over a thousand years earlier (*opposite*)

11

The Grosvenor Bridge (1827–32) at Chester, by Thomas Harrison, with the largest stone span (200 feet) in Britain.

Royal Institute of British Architects, the Society of Antiquaries, and the London Library. To the librarians and staff of all of these I am particularly grateful.

The suggestion for the book came from Dr Geoffrey Eley, to whom I here tender my thanks for his helpful advice and appreciation. To the publishers I am also thankful for their care over all aspects of production, and to Miss Sandra Wake for her research on the illustrations. Finally the book owes a great deal to my wife for her assistance at all stages and particularly with the proofs.

JOHN H. HARVEY

CHAPTER ONE
Man the Builder

Men have been builders for many hundreds of years, and in the modern civilized world most of us live in buildings. In what are called the under-developed countries many people still move about from place to place instead of being settled in one permanent home. We think of the Bedouin Arabs and, until quite recently, of many of the Red Indians of North America. Long ago a very large proportion of the human race wandered in this way, hunting wild animals and gathering food from wild plants. Civilization, which is the art of living in cities, developed as men more and more took to a life fixed in one place, taming some kinds of animals and growing plants for food. As soon as they settled in one place instead of moving on, it became convenient to make a permanent home rather than to live in a tent or in caves or other natural shelters which might be found at each stopping place. The story of civilization is then the story of building.

It is likely that one of the main reasons for stopping instead of moving on was the belief that some places were holy: that a certain spring or lake or river or hill was the favourite home of a god. We may not understand this belief, but the belief not only has been held for many centuries, but still is held by millions of people. Almost all men, at all periods of history, have felt that their luck was bound up with and depended upon the fortunes of their tribal or national god. If the god was made comfortable and received praise and sacrifices, he would in return look after his own people. For this reason temples were made at the holy places, as homes for the gods who lived there. These temples were probably the first buildings, or at any rate the first of any size or importance. At first only the unseen gods used these houses; then the priests who sang their praises and made sacrifices also lived in the temples. Finally the comfort and pleasure of living in a permanent shelter, specially made for convenience, led ordinary men and women to copy the temples on a smaller scale. Houses then were temples simplified.

In the course of many hundreds of years a great many improvements were made in the skills needed to make temples and houses. It is the story of this development that forms the history of the building crafts: each craft a way of solving problems of how to do it. Every temple or house has to be made out of materials; they have to be found, brought together, and shaped; then assembled to form the building. The kinds of materials used depended, to begin with, upon the place. If the country had many trees, it was easy to cut them down and shape them into posts and beams; and to fill up the spaces with smaller branches, twigs and brushwood. The roof could be covered with bunches of straw or reed or heather and other tough plants. In other countries, where there were few trees, blocks of stone could be quarried out of the ground; or clay could be dug and shaped into bricks which were dried in the sun or burnt in a kiln. Brick, and thin tiles of various shapes for the roof, are really an artificial stone.

There is a big difference between these two main sorts of material: the timber of trees is organic, or living; stones and clay are inorganic. Because living things reproduce themselves, or can be made to yield crop after crop, they need never become exhausted. If all buildings had been made from trees and other plants, and enough fresh forests and plantations had been made to keep up the stocks used, there would always be the material for the job. Quarries of stone and pits of clay, on the other hand, become worked out, and new sources of material have to be found. This is why the very large buildings of modern times are made of new materials. Concrete, glass, metals, synthetic fibres, are all used as substitutes for the natural materials which are becoming exhausted. There are, of course, other reasons for using these materials: some have greater strength than the natural timber or stone; others are admired for their appearance.

Rebuilding of the town of Utrecht, from *Fasciculus temporum*, made at Utrecht, 1480. Artist: John Veldener.

The appearance of buildings brings in another vital factor: design. A building, whether it is a temple or a house, a shop or a factory, is made for a particular purpose, and can be merely useful. But many men ask for more than this: they prefer one shape or colour or material to another. To please this taste or preference they ask that the building should be not only useful but also beautiful. Each separate building has then to be not simply built out of the materials to hand, but designed in advance to be of a certain shape and size, with its height in a definite proportion to its length and breadth, and doors and windows in given positions. The materials may be varied, to avoid monotony, and different colours chosen by the use of several stones or bricks, or laid on with paints. It is this settling of the shape and details and colour of the building in advance that is called Architecture. Each new house sets fresh questions to which answers have to be found. This is the difference between architecture and building, which consists of knowing the right answers to old questions.

Most of the large and important buildings of the last four or five thousand years have been deliberately designed: they are works of architecture. Here again we meet with the idea of what is holy, because men have always thought of creation—the making of something new—as a prerogative of gods. For this reason there are many stories of designers and architects receiving the pattern of what they were to build as a divine gift. Either they believed that a god had appeared to them in a dream to show them the correct design, or they felt that some accidental happening was really meant as a message from their god.

Beliefs like these had a great share in deciding the course taken by building. All purposeful design has to be based on measurement, and the knowledge of measures and of proportion—the relation of one measure to another—is geometry. God as creator of the world was imagined as a superman wielding an immense pair of compasses. It was held that man should imitate the Creator, yet not too closely. If he began to feel that his work of art was perfect, it was advisable to scratch or bruise it slightly so that it might not enter into rivalry with the handiwork of God. All the same, it was realized that man had a special talent denied to the animals, of choosing to impart an individual character to the things he made. Some beasts are notable builders, for example the beaver; almost all birds build nests. But the dams of beavers and the nests of birds have no private quality of design that marks one from another. The beaver and the blackbird work by an instinct which does not depend upon education and which produces more or less uniform results.

The buildings of man are never merely instinctive: all of them contain an element of purpose. But, as we have seen, they can be sharply divided into two great classes. On the one hand are simple buildings made according to more or less standard patterns and by traditional methods. These methods were handed down from father to son or from master to pupil in each of the skilled crafts. In each country or region the materials, the methods and the traditions built up were different. Yet within one district there was a great likeness between, for instance, all small farmhouses. To that extent, ordinary buildings are intermediate between the instinctive works of animals and the fully personal works of architecture designed one by one. It is impossible to divide all buildings sharply into the two classes: all works of architecture have a great deal of building tradition, and most buildings have at least a little of intentional design.

Design is never completely free from outside influences. The materials available in any given place and the traditional methods used there have always tended to shape design to some extent. The particular shapes pleasing to individuals, the architects themselves or the people for whom they worked, have been even more important. All the great changes that have taken place in the course of building history have been due mainly to the two factors of invention and fashion. The architect has been the inventor of new methods, finding fresh answers. His client, that is the person for whom the building is put up, promotes the spread of his architect's way of designing by recommending it to his friends. If the client was an emperor or king or high-priest or pope it was likely that there would be a fashion for that special kind of design.

In the search for new answers architects have

often looked at old buildings and buildings in other countries. From them they have obtained ideas and, with or without direct copying, have given the old or strange forms a fresh lease of life. Sometimes the borrowing has been quite intentional. In the eighteenth century English cabinet-makers designed "Chinese" furniture. At various periods architects have copied Roman, or Greek or Ancient Egyptian buildings, and through the nineteenth century many of them tried to use the style of the Middle Ages in what is called the Gothic Revival. In talking of "style" we have to distinguish it from fashion. Fashion is what is liked by influential people at a given time, and is usually short-lived. Style may last for many centuries and can include a number of fashions, one after another. All the fashions of one style are, however, related to each other like the members of a single family. The changes from one style to another depend upon fresh invention or upon rediscovery.

All the early styles were both national and religious. That is to say that the forms of building were peculiar to one single nation and derived from the temples of its gods. The main styles of this kind developed in ancient Egypt, Mesopotamia and Greece, as well as in India and China in the East, and in Peru and Mexico in America. The rise of great empires always meant that one style tended to spread outwards and to swallow up the lesser styles of conquered tribes. In some cases there was also an influence in the other direction, as when the Romans learned from Greece. Apart from the prehistoric monuments of standing stones and of posts, explored by modern archaeologists, there are no remains of architecture in Britain earlier than the first century AD. Only the Roman style, which then reached this country, was represented in our oldest real buildings. The

Monastic cell, Skellig Michael, Ireland. The original monastery at Iona must have been of this type. (*opposite*).

Roman methods of craftsmanship are the first that we can study seriously on home ground.

Craft Methods

The various styles of building were based upon different methods, and these were divided according to the main material used. We saw that materials are of two great classes: the living or organic, such as timber and thatch; and the inorganic, like stone and tile. The natures of the two classes are opposite. Timber grows lengthwise and is strong in tension—that is, it can be used as a tie to pull together walls which are being forced apart; stone, brick and tile, on the contrary, are used as blocks strong in compression—they resist great weights placed upon them. Each of these classes gave rise to a form of building construction. From timber, used as upright posts crossed by level beams, all the trabeated (beamed) forms of building are derived. Even the temples of ancient Greece, though built of stone or marble, show by their forms that they were copied from timber structures. We can see evidence of the same kind at Stonehenge, our one real building of prehistoric times, where large stones have been used as if they were posts and beams, and jointed as though they were wood.

The other great class, using mostly small pieces of stone or brick, lays one upon another and employs various devices to cover in the space between walls. The simplest method was to lay each course above a certain height slightly inward from the one below, so that eventually the courses from opposite sides met in the middle. If this was done over a building round in plan, a "beehive" shape was made. By cutting away the projecting edges of each course to form a smooth surface inside, a "dome" or a "vault" was made. These words are not in fact used to describe roofs made by this crude method of corbelling (bracketting) course upon course. It was found that if the stones or bricks were wedge-shaped, they could be laid so that (when finished) they all held each other in position by pressure. On a round plan, this made a real dome; over a square or parallel sided plan the result was a vault. A narrow piece of vault, the thickness of a wall, made an arch. From the use of the arch this whole class of building gets its name of arcuated (arched) construction.

All the oldest styles of architecture were either built of timber or copied from wooden originals. The arch was a much later invention, due to scarcity of trees and almost certainly first used in Mesopotamia (Iraq). There the earliest arches were of brick, but the idea was turned into stone and taken to Italy by the Etruscans, a mysterious people who moved westwards from the Near East. Roman building, though it was in many ways like that of Greece, differed completely in being based upon the arch, learned by the Romans from their neighbours the Etruscans. Many of the forms of Roman architecture were, all the same, taken from wooden originals. So it was in Roman times that the first style of mixed origin—based on the use of stone, brick and timber—came into being. It was this Roman style that was carried all over the western world as province after province was conquered for the Roman Empire.

Luckily we know almost everything about Roman methods of building, because a Roman architect named Vitruvius wrote an encyclopaedia of architecture (including engineering and all kinds of building skills), and many copies of it were made. Until recent times it was the only really complete book (in fact ten books in one) that had ever been written about building. For this reason it was one of the first books to be printed and from the sixteenth century was studied a great deal. The ruined buildings of ancient Rome were measured and drawn and were found to agree with the statements about design and method made by Vitruvius. It was this combination of study of ancient buildings with the surviving textbook that made the Renaissance (the rebirth of the ancient Roman style) possible in the fifteenth and sixteenth centuries.

Vitruvius described one by one the various materials used in building: brick, sand, lime, stone, timber, and the ways of using them. He gave valuable advice, for example as to the best time of year to make bricks, and ways of testing stone by leaving it in the open for two years. What was damaged after this was to be used only in the foundations below ground level. Although a great many skilled points of this kind were known to Vitruvius, who was both a designer and a master builder, he was not concerned with the passing on of the many precise details of craftsmanship. These were taught, generation after generation, by masters to their pupils in each craft.

Vernacular Building

Since buildings are not necessarily works of architecture, confusion often arises between building that is simply the result of tradition, and works which are the outcome of deliberate design. The purely traditional products of craft skills, mostly seen in country farmhouses, cottages, barns and other agricultural buildings, are called for distinction "Vernacular" buildings. The word is derived from the Latin *verna* which meant a slave born in his master's house, but was later used for anybody or anything home-born or home-grown (a vernacular language is the language of the place, as English is in England or Welsh in Wales).

Although it is important to keep in mind this distinction between the two great classes of building, most actual structures, even small houses or barns, owe something to architects as well as a lot to the traditionally trained craftsmen who built them. In the course of this book we shall be dealing mainly with the larger buildings designed by architects, but in every period there was a background of vernacular houses for the ordinary man and woman to live in, though few of them earlier than the fifteenth century now remain. From time to time the skilled craftsmen who built these ordinary small houses learned some new invention from the architects. It was by this indirect and slow process that vernacular style itself changed, and did not stay exactly the same century after century.

Bearing in mind that the very earliest timber buildings still standing in this country date from the thirteenth century, (except for part of Greensted Church, Essex—see pp. 27–8) it is easy to grasp that a lot must have happened by then. Even the most traditional buildings would have developed considerably in the course of five or six hundred years, the period since the Anglo-Saxons had taken possession of practically the whole of England. All the same, it cannot be an accident that there is a very big difference between the methods of timber framing used in south-eastern and in north-western England. In the south-east roofs were made with pairs of small rafters spaced about a foot or so apart, without any lengthwise ridgepiece at the top. The north-western part of the country always had a ridge supported upon pairs of heavy curving timbers called "crucks", and the smaller (common) rafters that bore the thatch were supported on the ridge at the top and on other timbers carried (lengthwise) by the crucks.

It is known for certain that Roman roofs were built with ridgepieces and also that they were used in Wales in the Dark Ages after the Romans had left. The earliest surviving roofs with ridgepieces are those in Wales and in the western half of England but in most of eastern England (as far north as Yorkshire and again in Northumberland) only roofs without ridgepieces are found. It is certain that, whatever may have been the actual periods, the date when the ridgeless roofs were first built is later than that of the earliest roofs with ridges. The only satisfactory explanation is that the ridgeless roofs are a quite different national method brought into England by an invasion from the Continent, and at a date before 1200. We cannot say that ridged roofs are Romano-British and ridgeless roofs Anglo-Saxon—they might be Norman or Flemish—but here we have in front of us the results of two different methods of work upon the same problem.

Hadrian's Wall, built in AD 122–26 across northern England from coast to coast; here seen in Northumberland.

The Dark Ages

Roman buildings in Britain were a foreign importation and apart from the walls of some forts (for example, at Pevensey and Portchester) and part of the wall of London, not very much of them remains above ground. The Roman bath at Bath, the amphitheatre at Caerleon, and the remains of Hadrian's Wall, as well as parts of several villas (Chedworth in Gloucestershire, Bignor in Sussex, and others) are among the most

interesting ruins, along with the *Pharos* or light-house in Dover Castle. This is generally considered the oldest building in Britain that is not a ruin and may belong to the first century.

Before going on to consider what is left of buildings of the Anglo-Saxon and Danish periods, a word must be said on the building of roads and bridges. We all know of the amazing roads built by the Romans across the whole of the Empire, from Persia to Britain, from Holland to Morocco. It was by the rapid movement of troops along these roads that the Romans were able for so long to rule so vast an area. The making of the roads involved surveying of the ground, the sighting of the straight alignments, and the actual forming of the road with drainage (to prevent water-logging) and surface. In the network of roads bridges to cross rivers and streams without delay were a vital need. Although we may feel that the roads themselves are not buildings, bridges certainly are.

Bridges were not just a practical matter: they were also a symbol. We know that the Pope is called a pontiff, and perhaps that this is the English form of the Latin word *pontifex*, which means a bridge-builder. The full title, *Pontifex Maximus* (Chief Bridge-builder) comes down for about 2,500 years. At first it meant the high priest of ancient Rome, who could be thought of as building a bridge between this world and the next. Later the emperors used the title, and when the Roman Empire died, it was taken by the popes who were the heads of the new religion. In Britain too bridge-building had a special place in the scheme of things. As far back as the eighth century, and probably earlier, the laws of the Anglo-Saxon kingdoms imposed three duties (often called the "Trinoda Necessitas") on every man: to serve in the army against invaders, to

The *Pharos* (lighthouse) in Dover Castle (1st century AD), the oldest substantially complete building to survive in Britain.

build and repair fortresses, and to build and repair bridges. In Saxon England all the bridges were of wood, and so were those of the Romans in Britain, though some of them had stone piers carrying timber beams. The first bridge of stone arches is said to have been the one across the river Lea east of London, at Stratford-le-Bow (of the arch). This was built soon after 1100 for Matilda, the queen of Henry I.

The remains of building before the coming of the Normans are practically limited to churches, and generally to towers or parts only. What is more, most of the churches that do survive belong to a very late date in the Saxon period. The few exceptions include parts of St. Martin's at Canterbury, the lonely chapel of St. Peter at Bradwell in Essex, built soon after 653; a large church at Brixworth, Northamptonshire, built about 670; and three churches in County Durham: Escomb, Monkwearmouth, and part of Jarrow. There are also underground crypts at Ripon and Hexham. Most of these are very plain, simple

St Peter's Chapel at Bradwell in Essex, built soon after 653, one of our few early Saxon churches.

The arches of Roman brick, now blocked, in Brixworth church originally provided a real basilica (*left*)

All Saints at Brixworth in Northamptonshire, another church begun in the 7th century (*below*)

The interior at Monkwearmouth, narrow and dark in a Dark Age. St Peter at Monkwearmouth in County Durham, founded in 674; the top stage of the tower is much later and shows improved stonework.

buildings, tall and narrow, and their walls are in imitation of late Roman building. St. Wilfrid is recorded to have brought masons from Rome itself to work at Hexham in 673–78, and Benedict Biscop who was in charge at Jarrow and Monkwearmouth called masons from Gaul (France) to build "in the manner of the Romans."

Most of the early Saxon churches and monasteries were destroyed by the Norsemen in their raids on this country in the eighth and ninth centuries. There are very many remains of later churches, but few of them are even nearly complete. There are many fine towers, including Sompting in Sussex with an unusual form of roof, and at Earl's Barton in Northamptonshire (built about the year 1000), where stone strips imitate timber framing. The best preserved of all churches is the one at Bradford-on-Avon in Wiltshire, solidly built and rather crude, but with a series of round arches used as decoration and reminding us of Roman architecture. Elsewhere many Saxon churches had small windows with triangular heads made by leaning two pieces of stone together, a very un–Roman device.

By the standards we are used to from looking at Norman and Gothic buildings, Saxon churches were very small. Until recently, the only cathedral plan known, from the ruined foundations, was at North Elmham in Norfolk. There the total length was only about 130 feet (40 metres). In the last ten years a much larger cathedral has been excavated at Winchester, to the north of the nave of the great Norman cathedral. At its largest this Saxon cathedral was 250 feet (75 metres) long, but it reached this only after great extensions made to east and west near the end of the tenth century. The original church of the seventh century was only about 100 feet (30 metres) long and quite narrow, under 25 feet (8 m) inside. The small size of all buildings, even those of the greatest importance, is also shown in the royal palace of Cheddar in Somerset. There the original Long Hall was only 78 feet by 20 (23 × 6 m) and when it was replaced by the first West Hall in the tenth century, this was even shorter (60 feet; 18 m), though it was about 30 feet across (9 m). These halls and all the other buildings of the Saxon palace were of timber.

At Greensted in Essex there remain the outer walls of the nave of the church, built about 1013. Although restored, the walls show what the construction was like. Oak logs were split in half and set upright along a level beam as a foundation, with the round sides outwards. This sounds very simple, but the carpentry was quite skilful. Each post was jointed with a tenon and pegs to the beams above and below, the foundation sill and the wallplate; and with a "tongue" fitted into grooves in each half trunk, so that there was a perfect wooden wall without cracks. This is believed to be the only remaining piece of timber construction in Britain that dates from before the

All Saints Church at Earl's Barton, Northamptonshire (about AD 1000), has stone strips imitating timber framing (*above*).

The Saxon church of St Lawrence at Bradford-on-Avon, Wiltshire, largely rebuilt in the tenth century.

The interior of Bradford-on-Avon consisted of separate compartments linked by small arches.

Norman Conquest, and even then it is only some fifty years earlier.

Since even cathedrals and royal halls of Saxon times were quite small, we can be sure that the houses of the time were mostly little more than huts. Only a very few thanes (noblemen) are likely to have had houses of substantial size, though we know that some buildings had upper storeys. St Dunstan, presiding over a meeting of the Witan (the Saxon parliament) at Calne in Wiltshire in 978, saved himself on a beam when the floor gave way and all the members fell into the basement. Even though the Witan may not have had a great many members, this must have been a large room, and need not mean that ordinary dwellings were either large or of more than one storey. The building of really large structures, forgotten in Britain since Roman times, had to wait until after 1066.

St Andrew's at Greensted, Essex, the only wooden building to survive from Saxon times (about 1013). The upright logs are skilfully jointed.

CHAPTER TWO

Norman Building

The change in buildings due to the Norman Conquest in 1066 was very great. The Norman style was already in fashion at the court of the Saxon king Edward the Confessor. He had lived in exile in Normandy for many years and realized the advantages of Norman civilization. So when he determined to rebuild Westminster Abbey in 1050, he chose the Norman style. The names of his architects are Saxon, but he may have sent them to study across the Channel. There were also Norman lords who received grants of land in England and Wales before 1065, and they too used the style of their own country. So the way had been prepared by the time that a Norman duke became king of England and his followers became lords and squires throughout the land.

The Norman way of building formed part of the Romanesque style, the version of late Roman art that ruled Western Europe in the eleventh century. It was different in appearance from the late Saxon work, and Norman churches and halls were far larger in many cases. A much greater proportion of all building was of stone, and private houses began to be built of stone for the first time. Also new were the Norman castles, at first earthen ramparts with timber palisades, but soon carrying great stone keeps. There is no space

Building of the 11th century, from Bodleian Library MS. Junius 11.

in this short book to describe castles and fortifications, but the point must be made that the Normans spent a great deal of the total revenue of England on this new and costly form of building, partly to defend the country from Norsemen and other invaders but also largely to overawe the Saxon population.

It is no exaggeration to say that the enormous building programme of 1066–1135 (from the Conquest to the death of Henry I) changed the face of England to an extent unequalled until canals and railways came seven and eight centuries later. The number and size of the greater churches and monasteries challenged comparison with the work of Roman times, seven centuries and more earlier. After such a long period of "thinking small" the transformation within a few years to an age of "building big" is almost unbelievable. This new architecture was the greatest revolution in the whole of English history. We have to try to understand why it happened and how all the work could be done.

The chief reason why it happened lies in the ambitious character of the Normans, who dominated the period. They had already conquered Sicily and southern Italy before taking England, and within a few years afterwards played an important part in the First Crusade. In order to succeed in their conquests, and to keep what they had won, the Normans developed the system of government and of taxation. The most famous evidence of this in England is Domesday Book, the detailed record of every place and how much it was worth. So the Normans had, only twenty years after the Conquest, complete knowledge of the land they had taken. In the same period they had put down rebellions and built castles, so that there was no hope of a new revolt by the Saxons. To build the castles they had had to find materials and skilled men, and had learned how to get materials across country to the place where they were needed. So, well before 1100, they had the organization to do the work.

The reason for building so many monasteries, many of them large, was rather different. Because of the bloodshed at the battle of Hastings, and in the later revolts after the Conquest, the Norman winners had guilty consciences. Though tough and ruthless, they were not the barbarians that their ancestors had been only a hundred years or so before. They were, many of them, sincerely religious men who wished to be famous for good as well as great deeds. They were taught by their priests that bloodthirsty warriors who did not repent were likely to go to Hell when they died. It would be a safeguard if they gave part of the land they had conquered, and some of their money, to the Church. Parish churches, endowed with glebe land for the priest, and with the tithes (tenths) of the produce from the land in the parish, were built by the lords for their tenants. Monasteries were given much larger grants so that they might encourage religion and pray for the souls of their founders day and night.

William the Conqueror and his queen Matilda set the fashion and, having founded two great abbeys, for monks and for nuns, at Caen in Normandy, also founded Battle Abbey on the site of the battle of Hastings. There the souls, not only of the royal founders, but of all the Saxons and Normans killed in the battle, would be safeguarded by perpetual prayers. Once the fashion had been set, lords and squires everywhere followed suit, and gave to religion an enormous share of their new estates. The king, as leader in the movement, favoured the new abbeys with great privileges. They were let off most forms of tax, and their land did not have to pay tithes. For over four hundred years they had a specially favoured position and later kings continued to make gifts and to grant privileges. So the monasteries were rich enough to build on a grand scale. The next question to answer is why they wished to build in this costly way.

Undoubtedly the main reason was the ambitious character of the Normans, already mentioned. But other factors were present. During the eleventh century there had already been a wave of large churches built in different parts of Europe. In the Dark Ages after the collapse of the Roman Empire men came to believe that the end of the world was coming at the "millenium," the thousandth year of the Christian era. When it was found that the world was still going on in 1001, everybody took a deep breath and began again, and in thankfulness they rebuilt churches everywhere. The new buildings were larger than the old ones, and in some cases were deliberately meant to be bigger than any others known. By the time of the Norman Conquest, a process of "keeping up with the Joneses" was well under way, and very large churches were models for still larger ones to be built.

The churches at great centres of pilgrimage imitated St. Martin at Tours, and each was built a little larger than the one before. In the north of France was the abbey of St. Remi at Rheims with a church begun in 1005 to be the largest in Gaul. The cathedral of Speyer in Germany was enormous. Finally, when the most famous monastery in Western Europe, at Cluny in Burgundy, came to be rebuilt after 1085 it was laid out on a bigger scale than anything that had gone before. On the Continent, however, there were already many quite large churches, so that there was less excuse for rebuilding them than in England. England gave an opportunity for experiment and lavish design that was unequalled anywhere else. Since the new Norman lords were able to pay the bill, and in fact eager to do so, the next fifty years saw an immense programme of work.

We talk of the Norman style, but it was really two styles, early and late. The whole period, in English building, lasted for about a hundred years from the first Norman work under Edward the Confessor until the first traces of the new Gothic style began to appear after 1150. In the middle, just after 1100, there was a great change in the methods of building. All the early work had been rough and crude, made with small stones rather badly cut, and put together with thick beds of lime mortar. The plans were irregular, because the builders were not at all accurate in geometry and did not set out true right angles of 90 degrees. Nobody knew any better because the works of Euclid had been lost and very few of the craftsmen had been trained in places where better methods were still known. For on the edges of Europe there were lands where the ancient knowledge of the Greeks and Romans lived on: in Byzantium (Istanbul), in the south of Spain under the Moors, and in Sicily. It was in Sicily that Normans had already conquered the Moors, but learned to live with them, and took advantage of their expert skills.

The fact that the Normans in England could build bigger and better than the Saxons, even at the start, was due to what they had learned from the Moors: directly in Sicily, and also indirectly through Italians who had learned from Moors in the south of Italy. Even so, the results were not very well made, and the chronicles tell of many early Norman towers and buildings that fell down. Then something happened that changed the picture altogether: the First Crusade of 1097–1099. The Franks (the people of western Europe who recognized the Pope as head of the Church)

B

invaded Turkey and Syria, beat the Turks and Arabs, and captured Jerusalem. For ninety years Jerusalem was the capital of a western kingdom in the Near East, surrounded by other states ruled by the Crusader Franks. From the first, within a few years of taking Jerusalem, Crusaders returned with new knowledge they had learned abroad. They also brought with them Saracen (Turkish, Arab and other eastern) prisoners of war. Many of them must have been military engineers who, in time of peace, were trained masons, carpenters, and artists.

We know that methods of building, about 1100, were much better in the Near East than in Western Europe. So it is not surprising that Crusaders could learn from their experiences, and bring back craftsmen more highly skilled than those at home. From about 1105 a new and very different sort of stonework can be seen in English buildings. Instead of small rough stones bedded in thick mortar, larger well-cut blocks with fine edges had extremely thin joints. It was even said that masonry of this new kind looked as if it were all in one piece. The larger stones could not easily be carried by one man in his hands, like the old ones, but needed cranes or other hoisting engines. The introduction of such machinery, and of stronger scaffolding, was also brought from the East and from southern Europe.

Most of the big new buildings, apart from castles, were churches or monasteries, but in 1097–99 Westminster Hall was built. The hall is 238 feet long by 68 feet wide inside, and was the largest room in the West for a hundred and fifty years, until St. Louis (Louis IX of France) built an even larger hall in Paris. Although much smaller than the largest halls of ancient Rome— the Basilica of Maxentius was 265 feet by 83 feet —Westminster Hall was vastly bigger than even the Hall of the Emperor at Goslar in Germany (only 145 by 45 feet). Norman ambition was not satisfied with anything less than first place. This was seen in the new cathedral at Winchester, entirely replacing the Saxon Old Minster, and even longer than the abbey church at Cluny. Bury St. Edmunds Abbey, even if not bigger than Cluny, was about the same size.

What is amazing about the building programme of the period is not merely the size of the largest buildings, but the great number of smaller ones. It has been reckoned that there were over ten thousand parishes in mediaeval England, and most of these had a church built or rebuilt, or altered, in Norman times. It is true that many were quite small, and were very much like each other. Standard patterns, built by gangs of masons moving across country, may account for this. But altogether the amount of building achieved in only two or three generations surpasses anything that can be found in other countries. Besides the churches and castles there were also stone houses in the bigger towns, but few of them now remain and most are in ruins. Several of them were built for wealthy Jews, for example in Bury St. Edmunds and in Lincoln. The Jews needed the protection of stone houses, not so much because they were unpopular, but because they were almost the only people (except for the abbots of the great monasteries) who kept large quantities of cash. A Jew's House like the famous one on Steep Hill in Lincoln was not just a dwelling, but also a bank.

The Norman cathedrals that remain were mostly begun after the death of William the Conqueror, but there are two important exceptions. These are St Albans, started in 1077, and Winchester whose foundations were laid two years later. We can see the crude strength of early Norman work at both of these, and contrast it

The Norman Jew's House in Lincoln was a bank as well as a house; it was built about 1175.

Durham (1093–1133) is the most perfect example of a Norman cathedral.

The Norman nave of Gloucester Abbey, begun in 1089 and now the Cathedral.

with later improvements. At St Albans the last Saxon abbots had been collecting tiles from the ruins of the Roman city of Verulamium, so that Paul, the first Norman abbot, was able to get off to a flying start. His architect, the famous Master Robert, was able to finish a large part of the church in eleven years. The much larger church at Winchester had to be built of stone brought from a distance but all the same a great part of it was completed in fourteen years and probably the whole in little over twenty. This may have been the result of too much hurry, for in 1107 the central tower fell and had to be rebuilt. It is the contrast between the original work and this rebuilding that shows, more clearly than anywhere else, the wonderful advance in skill within a few years.

The later Norman cathedrals, begun in the 1090s, were not finished until well into the twelfth century. They benefited from the new developments and begin to show new inventions. At Gloucester it must have been meant from the start to build a high stone vault and hidden flying buttresses were made above the lower vaults of the aisles. At Durham the chronicles tell us exactly how long the different parts of the cathedral took to build. It was started on 11th August 1093; the choir was vaulted in stone and the wooden centres were taken down by 4th September 1104. The nave, to the west of the central crossing and transepts, had been begun in 1099 and was not finished until 1128. Its vault, which still stands, was built in the five years from 1128 to 1133. The choir vault was later rebuilt as we see it, and additions were made at east and west ends, but Durham remains the most perfect example of a complete Norman cathedral. It is important in architectural history because its vaults were the first to be built on stone ribs. This became, thirty years or so later, one of the principal marks of the Gothic style, as we shall see.

The other really large Norman churches were mostly in the eastern part of England: Ely, Norwich and Peterborough. There was also the vast church of Old St Paul's in London, the biggest of all until it was burnt in the Great Fire of 1666. In drawings made by Wenceslaus Hollar before the fire we can still see its grand Norman nave, a later work than most of the other Norman cathedrals and so probably the finest of them all. The improvement in cutting stone and in finishing details went on, so that after the middle of the twelfth century buildings had quite lost the crudity of sixty years before. Many new forms of decoration, including most of the elaborate zig-zags and other patterns which we see on Norman arches, had been adopted. The zigzag in particular had been brought back from the Near East by Crusaders. So had other tricks of construction, like the "joggled" stones of flat arches which were used above fireplaces.

Mention of the fireplace takes us back to the few remaining Norman houses, most of which date from rather late in the period, about 1140 or later. They were sometimes quite large, like the ruined one at Southampton, and had at least two storeys. In fact it was the rule for the main living rooms to be on an upper floor above store–rooms or, in the towns, shops at ground level; and perhaps standing above vaulted cellars underground. Though few houses were built of stone throughout, a great many had stone cellars and some had masonry walls to the ground storey with a timbered upper stage above. The danger of fire was great, and the chronicles record fires again and again in London and most other cities and towns.

London has preserved a remarkable set of

Inside Durham Cathedral, showing the vaults built cn stone ribs, the earliest instance of this characteristic Gothic technique. (*above*)
The nave of Norwich Cathedral, finished abou 1145, shows the improvement in masonry sinc the earlier Gloucester (*below*).

regulations about building, dated in 1189, called the "London Assise." This shows not only the detailed care with which various structural and legal problems were considered before the end of the twelfth century, but also tells us something of the earlier Norman period. "It is to be remembered that of old times the greater part of the city was built of timber and the houses covered with straw and stubble and the like thatch; so that when one house was set on fire most of the City was burnt, as happened in the first year of the reign of King Stephen (1136) . . . Afterwards many of the citizens, trying to avoid such a risk as best they could, built on their foundations a stone house covered with thick tiles." So we know that the general run of houses in early Norman times were wooden, but that later, especially after this great fire of London in 1136, there was a big change towards building in stone, and with tiled roofs instead of thatch.

From Domesday Book a lot can be learnt about the numbers of houses in towns, but not much of their size and plan. Calculations show that the plots were broad in early times and so had houses built sideways on to the street. Later the plots were divided lengthwise, so that two or three houses might share the frontage, and then they were built with their narrow gable ends to the street, and perhaps a narrow courtyard stretching back along the plot behind the house. On these town plots several small houses or cottages might later on be built along the courtyard, besides the chief house near the street. At first the cottages might be for servants of the occupier of the big house, but later they were generally occupied by tenants who paid a rent. The need to make full use of the cramped sites squeezed inside the protection of the city walls caused overcrowding to get worse and worse as time went on.

Even in Norman times there were suburbs outside the cities. Some of them sprang up as scattered houses were built on plots along the main roads coming in to the gates. Some of these would be inns for travellers and others would be shops and smithies where horses could be shod. A great deal of such building was quite haphazard. But we learn, again from Domesday Book in its account of Lincoln, that a planned development on open land had taken place before 1086. One Colswein, a Saxon, but evidently in the Norman king's favour, had a great many estates scattered about Lincolnshire. Also, "outside the city (of Lincoln) he has 36 houses and 2 churches which he built on the waste land that the king gave him and that was never before built upon." This sounds remarkably like a garden city or a speculative housing estate.

We have to picture at least two generations of frantic activity. All over the country old towns were being rebuilt, new churches were going up, monasteries gigantic in comparison with any institutions of Saxon times were planned and erected. Large numbers of men, as skilled craftsmen and as labourers, must have been employed, and in some cases were moved from job to job. For many of the larger buildings in the south of England, stone was imported in boats from the quarries at Caen in Normandy. In other cases local quarries had to be opened and worked on a far bigger scale than ever before. Timber, for framed buildings and for all roofs and scaffolding, had to be found, felled, and carried to the site or to the carpenter's yard. Some of the journeys were very long indeed, for we hear that the Abbot of Abingdon soon after 1100 was sending to Wales for beams and rafters. "He had six wains and twelve oxen to each of them. The journey coming and going, as far as Shrewsbury (about 220 miles return) took six or seven weeks.''

This great campaign of building lasted through the reigns of the first three Norman kings, William the Conqueror and his sons William Rufus and Henry I. After Henry's death in 1135 the country was plunged into civil war and anarchy for twenty years, and it was only in the reign of Henry II (1154–1189) that architecture again became a preoccupation. By that time style had changed and was what is now called Transitional. This is because it shares the characteristics and details of the Norman work that had gone before, and of the new Gothic which was to take its place. Before going on to consider Gothic buildings, we must see what was happening in the thirty-five years of rule by the great king Henry, the first of the Angevin or Plantagenet line.

The end of the Norman dynasty, the civil wars, and the coming of Henry from Anjou with his young queen Eleanor of Aquitaine, combined to have a great effect upon building. The fact that Henry, and still more his queen, came from further south than Normandy, gave them quite a different outlook. Henry's close relatives were kings of Jerusalem and Eleanor's family ruled over a great region that was under the influence of Spain and the Mediterranean. Refinements in art, literature and civilization, not expected in Norman times, were becoming the rule. Towards the end of the twelfth century this became very obvious in architecture. Just as there had been a big change soon after 1100 from crudity towards greater precision and accuracy, so a second wave about 1160 took matters a stage further.

While England had been in the throes of civil war the leadership of the West had passed to the kingdom of France. France, with its capital Paris, was then quite a small country, but its kings were trying to become masters of the whole of ancient

Gaul, the area that we know as France today. Though many centuries were to pass before their aim was achieved, France even in the limited sense was a leading power under its kings Louis VI and Louis VII. So far as concerned architecture, they were nobly served by the great abbot of the royal monastery of St-Denis, Suger. Suger had been at school with Louis VI and for two years lived in Rome with Pope Calixtus II. He knew King Henry I of England also, and was on friendly terms with most of the great men of the time. When he was made abbot of St-Denis in 1122 he began to plan a thorough rebuilding of the abbey. By 1140 he had completed a new west front and there used on a large scale the ribbed vault and the pointed arch. The pointed arch, which completely alters the style of buildings, had been brought from the Near East, where it had been in use among the Arabs, Persians and Turks for three hundred years.

Then came the great breakthrough, the change from the heavy and solid Romanesque way of building to strong but light walling of far better quality. So far as we know, the very first work in Europe to use this improved method was the east end of St-Denis built for Suger. As at Durham, we are lucky in having an exact record of the dates when this was built: it started on 14th July 1140 and was brought to an end on 11th June 1144. The beginning of the Gothic style goes back to those years, but it was a long time before it was fully adopted. As at all such changes, many people were conservative and preferred the old type of building that they knew. In England, as we have just seen, political conditions meant that the time was not ripe for important artistic change. So for about fifty years the period of the Transition lasted, with the new style and its methods slowly displacing the old. It was not until well after 1200 that the

Man building a wall from *Robert the Devyll*. Printed by Wynkyn de Worde, ?1517.

41

Canterbury Cathedral
choir was rebuilt in
1174–84 in the early
Gothic style brought
from France by
William of Sens.

use of the round arch was completely displaced by the pointed arches of the Gothic style.

There are several good examples of Transitional style in the English cathedrals. Soon after 1154 Ripon Minster was begun, and parts of its nave can still be seen. Then about 1170 came the western "Galilee" porch added to Durham Cathedral. There the slender piers and light character of the work are Gothic, but the round arches still look Norman. At the west end of Ely Cathedral a transept and tower were built between 1174 and 1197; and a similar extension (now hidden behind the west front) was made at Peterborough about 1177–1193. Across the country at Worcester Cathedral there was another western extension, looking decidedly Gothic but with a mixture of old-fashioned detail. Looking at any of these, we can sense the struggle going on in the minds of the designers, pulled one way by their training, but led towards a new fashion that had fired men's imagination.

What was happening in France was well known in England, and when the choir of Canterbury Cathedral was burnt down in 1174 the monks sent abroad for an architect. There seems even to have been some sort of competition, and it was won by a Frenchman, William of Sens. He almost certainly came from Sens, where the first complete Gothic cathedral had just been finished. In four seasons from 1175 to 1178, this French architect rebuilt the choir and eastern transepts before he was seriously injured by falling from the scaffold. His English assistant, another William, then built the east end in 1179–1184 in an even more advanced style. Yet all this work at Canterbury still had much about it that smacked of the old: columns that were almost Roman, and zigzag mouldings that looked Norman. The turn of genuine English Gothic was still to come.

CHAPTER THREE

Gothic Builders

The technical developments in the methods of building after 1100 and of the formation of the Gothic style had come near to perfection by the end of the twelfth century. In France and in England there were architects, mostly master masons, who could design and build on a grand scale. Their works, though often large and complex, seldom fell down. They were completely in charge and knew very well what they were doing, so that buildings in Gothic style look satisfactory and well finished where the earlier Norman work had often seemed raw and rough. Gothic was the style of a very high civilization that was no longer primitive in any sense.

England under Henry II was a prosperous country that had recovered from the civil wars and enjoyed a "Golden Age" that has been called "The Twelfth-Century Renaissance." Unlike the later Renaissance it did not seek to imitate Roman art directly, but art and science were influenced by the new translations of ancient Greek and Latin books. The Greek philosophers and scientists had been forgotten in the West, but in the East their books had been turned into Arabic in the ninth century. Most of the new translations were actually made into Latin from the Arabic and not from the Greek. This meant that the

The interior of Wells
Cathedral: the stairs to
the Chapter House.

Aerial view of Wells
Cathedral, the first to be
designed (about 1180) in a
completely Gothic style.

translators had to work in close touch with Arabs
and with people (many of them Spaniards) who
knew Arabic as well as their own language. This
was important for building as well as for learning
and explains how eastern ideas of design and
decoration come to be found in England. There
is a special reason too for connecting English
architecture with eastern methods. A Welsh
chronicle tells that a Saracen mason called "Lalys"
was brought back a prisoner from Palestine, and
built Neath Abbey. He also became architect to
Henry I (before 1135) and "taught the art to many
of the Welsh and English."

It is striking that the first truly Gothic style in
England is not the French importation at Canterbury, for that has still much that smacks of the
Roman and the Norman. Independently in the
West of England and in South Wales there was a
new style which appeared in the nave of Worcester
Cathedral, already mentioned. Soon afterwards a
whole cathedral, at Wells in Somerset, was designed in this pure Gothic. Except for the use of
pointed arches in both Canterbury and Wells,

Wells was designed in an English manner
traditional in the western counties.

there is hardly any similarity between them. Something from Canterbury went to the design of the new cathedral at Lincoln, whose choir and transepts were built in 1192–1200. From then on the whole of the thirteenth century was filled with great achievements in architecture.

The great buildings of the period, built in what is called the Early English style, include not only large parts of the cathedrals at Lincoln, Ely, Peterborough and Chichester, but also the whole of Salisbury (1220–1266) and the great transepts at York Minster. At Salisbury the city as well as the cathedral was built afresh on a clear site, because Old Sarum was too cramped and had no proper water supply. The new city was regularly planned in blocks and had an ample water supply running in canals through the streets. Although so many of the houses have been rebuilt again and again, we can still get some idea of a city of the middle of the thirteenth century at Salisbury. The cathedral in the middle of its green close, surrounded by the houses of the canons and other church officials, is the living record of another quieter world than ours.

Besides the cathedrals, many abbeys were built or rebuilt. The work of the Early English period is more seen in the great ruined monasteries than any other. Although it was not possible to find the money to pull down and rebuild all the immense Norman buildings, it is amazing how much was done. Chief of all these works was the rebuilding of Westminster Abbey for King Henry III, beginning with a new Lady Chapel where the later Henry VII's Chapel now stands, and going on through the rest of the Middle Ages. In Yorkshire alone there were the great churches at Byland, Rievaulx and Whitby Abbeys, at Bolton and Bridlington Priories, and a great part of Beverley Minster. In the south was Netley

The east end of Lincoln Cathedral chapter house.

Lincoln Cathedral, begun for St Hugh in 1192, is a superb achievement in the Early English style.

Abbey; in the west were Pershore and Tintern. In every part of the country remains of this time can be seen.

Among the smaller parish churches too a great deal was done, but a far larger proportion of them was rebuilt in the later Gothic styles of the fourteenth and fifteenth centuries. The Early English work at its best can be recognized by the use of the tall narrow "lancet" window. As yet there was little use of tracery, though it was brought in by Henry III in his royal works and at Westminster Abbey. Columns and piers were often surrounded by tall slender shafts, and these had sharply moulded bases and capitals with fine carving, often of leaves, but also with heads, sometimes meant to be comic. The heavy mouldings of Norman arches were superseded by elegant series of fine mouldings, and the zigzag gave place to the "dogtooth" ornament. This is like a row of small pyramids, generally cut into little "petals."

Gothic Methods

We have seen that even in the middle of the Norman period there was a great improvement in the skills of the building craftsmen. Improvement continued until after 1200 but by the middle of the thirteenth century the builders had learned all the technical devices, which they were to use for several centuries. It was not, in fact, until the nineteenth century that there were any important advances in the way that buildings were erected. To give some idea of what was done, let us consider a typical building of the time and the various stages of work that went to produce Gothic architecture.

First of all the house or church or castle had to be designed. According to the needs of the client who wanted it built a plan had to be made. This might not necessarily be on a sheet of paper or parchment, but could be worked out on a boarded floor or even measured on the ground to full size. From a given base-line a right-angle would have to be set up by measuring a triangle with sides in the proportions of 3, 4 and 5. Once this had been done, either to a small scale or on the ground, the rest of the plan would follow by using methods of proportion and counting units. Trenches were dug along the lines settled for the walls, and pits where columns were to stand. Into the trenches and pits rough stone would be tipped, and flooded with lime mortar to make a concrete foundation. In wet marshy ground a deeper foundation might be made by driving wooden piles down in rows and then fastening level planks on top of them. The piles were driven down with a ram, a very heavy log hoisted by means of a pulley and then allowed to fall onto the top of the pile. The bottom end of each pile had to be sharpened, and was often shod with an iron point made by a

The interior of Lincoln impresses by its perfect proportions and clarity of detail (*top*).

Westminster Abbey, rebuilt for King Henry III after 1245 (*far left*).

The whole of Salisbury Cathedral, except tower and spire, was built between 1220 and 1266 (*left*).

blacksmith. Elm was the best wood for piles, but oak, beech and alder were used too,

On top of the concrete or plank foundation the first course of hewn stone would be laid. At this stage would come the ceremony of laying the first stone, which might come several years after works had started. In the case of churches it was usual for the "foundation stone" to be laid by the bishop, but sometimes a number of stones was laid by different notable people. At Salisbury Cathedral in 1220 the bishop laid three stones: one for the Pope, one for the Archbishop of Canterbury, and one for himself. The Earl and Countess of Salisbury then laid the fourth and fifth stones, and more were set by other noblemen and by the Dean, the Precentor, Chancellor and Treasurer of the cathedral; by the archdeacon and each of the canons present. Other noblemen who were away with Henry III fighting the Welsh on the border paid a visit to Salisbury on their return from campaign, and added more stones.

It appears that financial contributions were expected from those who laid foundation stones, and this was just one of the ways in which funds were raised. Collectors were sent round the diocese to raise money for the building of a cathedral, and appeals went out. Many people left money in their wills, hoping that their names would be included in the list of benefactors who would be prayed for regularly when the church was finished. Sometimes, though not very often, people actually helped the work with their own hands. All classes of society, from noblemen and their wives down to labourers, did this at times, but as they were unskilled they generally could do little more than push a wheelbarrow or help in some other way to carry materials.

The skilled men were divided into gangs according to their different crafts, but all of them came under the orders of the master mason as architect. In charge of each gang was a foreman and when the master was away from the building his place was taken by the warden of the masons, whose work was equivalent to that of a site architect in modern times. The first gang on the site would be the labourers and excavators, who cleared a level space and dug the foundation trenches. In many cases, particularly when building castles, town walls, the walls round cathedral closes, or large manorhouses, they would also dig a surrounding ditch and throw the earth up inside it to form a rampart. Meanwhile supplies of stone and lime had been arranged by the master, who generally visited the quarries to select sound beds of stone. In some cases, where suitable stone could not be had locally, diagrams marked on sheets of canvas were sent away (sometimes overseas to Caen) so that stones could be cut to size at the quarry and save some of the cost of transport.

Working masons were taken on in sufficient numbers for the size of the job. For the king's works and sometimes for other great buildings, masons and other craftsmen were impressed, that is conscripted. They were given "prest" money for their journey calculated on the number of miles they would be on the road, and told to report for duty. In ordinary cases men who were out of a job simply asked for work and were taken on if they could show the warden or foreman that they understood their craft. In the case of large jobs with a great many unknown men there was a risk of heavy losses by spoiling materials. This applied particularly to masonry, and this was the reason for using masons' marks.

For many hundreds of years marks had been used by masons, each mark indicating the man who made it as if it were a signature. When fully trained a mason was allotted a mark or allowed

Tomb-slab of Master William de Wermington, mason, of Croyland Abbey, Lincolnshire, who died *c.* 1350. Note compasses and a small square.

49

to choose one, and it was often only slightly different from the mark his father had used before him. If he worked on a small job near home, where all the gang of men were known to the foreman, there might be no need to cut personal marks. Every mason was considered competent to do sound work. But in a very big building with dozens of strange masons, impressed from a distance, the only safe way to put the responsibility for unsatisfactory work where it belonged was to insist that each man should put his personal mark on every stone he cut. If two men had the same mark, the younger man would have to use a fresh mark allotted to him while he was there, but on another job could go back to his original mark.

The stones had to be roughly shaped only in the case of rubble walling. For more important buildings with ashlar walling every stone had to be cut to a true flat face on the front and on both ends as well as the top and bottom "beds". Sound masons always kept the finished stone the right way up (that of the natural bed in the quarry) and except for long pieces of vertical shafting, never set the level beds upright. The front face of the stone which would show on the surface of the wall was "tooled". This meant that the edge of the chisel or of a special tool had to be driven across the surface to form a regular pattern. In some cases this might take the form of small pits and in others of grooves from side to side, from the top of the stone to the bottom, or slantwise. The slantwise form called "diagonal tooling" was used in Norman times and for most of the twelfth century. Afterwards the grooves tended to be smaller and smaller and by the end of the Middle Ages it was common to drag them with a piece of sawblade from a smalltoothed saw.

The masons who cut the stones worked on a bench or "banker" inside a hut or shelter. This shed was called the "lodge" and was used for eating meals and for rest and discussion as well as for working. At the cathedrals and larger buildings such as royal castles and palaces, where maintenance work was always going on, there would be a permanent lodge with a few men. If a large new addition was to be made to the building, a new lodge might be built with a separate staff. In some cases there were two masters, one for the old work in charge of routine, and the other who was architect for the newly designed addition. The master did not usually work in the lodge but in his "tracing house" where drawings were made. In the tracing house there would be drawing boards on trestles, and part of the floor was often laid with a slab of plaster of Paris. On the slab large drawings could be made by scratching. This produced clean white lines on the grubby grey surface. When the drawing was finished with it was only necessary to sweep the floor to dirty the lines and so leave it ready for a fresh drawing. Two of these plaster floors, covered with a confusing mass of lines from many drawings, exist at Wells Cathedral and at York Minster.

As soon as the walls had risen about five feet from the ground it would be impossible to go on laying courses of stone without a scaffold. So supplies of timber for scaffolding and a gang of carpenters used to making it would have to be brought onto the site. There were several kinds of scaffold used in the Middle Ages. The simplest, which could be used where the stones were small and the weight slight at any one time, consisted of long poles laid through the wall and simply bracketed out on each side. On the poles were laid wicker hurdles, tied down with ropes. A much stronger scaffold, needed for large heavy stones, was made in the modern way with poles some way out from the wall and crosspieces, called "putlogs," lashed to the poles at the outer end and inserted in putlog-holes left in the wall. A third kind of scaffold, especially used in building round towers, was the spiral scaffold, where the poles stuck out from the wall like very shallow steps in a spiral staircase, and hurdles were laid on a slope.

Ladders were used to get up the ordinary kinds of scaffold. Some were like modern ladders but others were made with just one tall beam drilled with holes through which the rungs were pushed to project on each side. (Short ladders of this sort are still often found in church belfries to climb onto the bell frame). As long as the early stonework of small pieces easily carried continued to be made, labourers carried them up ladders one by one or in baskets. Larger stones had to be wound up on ropes with a pulley and several kinds of cranes were used. The ordinary kind was worked with a windlass, two or more workmen pushing spokes instead of a handle. In this case the men were on the ground. For heavy loads that had to be taken to the top of the great cathedrals or towers, a large treadmill wheel was built, usually high up in the roof. Such wheels exist at Canterbury, Salisbury and Peterborough Cathedrals, where they were used for raising the bells after their use on the building work was over.

Arches had to be built on wooden centres made by the carpenters to the right shape according to the master's drawings. In some cases the centres were carried on temporary beams laid on the capitals of the piers or columns. At other times they had to be supported on struts from the floor or even on a very strong scaffolding when the high vaults of a large church were to be built. After each arch had set firmly, the timber centre could be taken down and used for the next arch of the same size. It was usual for the timber roofs which carried the tiles or lead to be built as soon as the walls were finished. The building could then begin to be used even if vaults were to be built, and the building could go on beneath the shelter of the roof.

In addition to the masons who cut the stones and laid them, and the carpenters who made the scaffolding, the centres, and the permanent roofs, there were men of other crafts. Blacksmiths were always needed, to sharpen the masons' tools regularly, and also to make iron bars to strengthen pinnacles, to tie together the sides of arches, and to provide grilles to protect windows. In the fourteenth century they sometimes made hidden bands of reinforcement. This has been found at Gloucester and Salisbury Cathedrals. Plumbers were needed to lay lead gutters and also the roofs of cast lead sheets which were used more and more as time went on. Many roofs continued to be laid with tiles and some with stone slates or thatch. Finally the decoration of the building might include wall paintings, and churches had their windows filled with stained glass. Most ordinary houses did without glass. Either the windows were left open by day and closed with wooden shutters at night, or they were screened with greased linen or sheets of greased paper. Such windows let light through, but it was not possible to look out of them. We have to remember that ordinary people in the Middle Ages spent most of the day outdoors and came home at night to eat and sleep.

The Architects

In charge of all this work were the masters, mostly master masons. In the case of timber-framed houses and important roofs the architect who designed the work was the master carpenter. In spite of the fact that many records have been lost and destroyed, many hundreds of names of mediaeval architects are known. The list starts with a few of the time of the Norman Conquest, and goes on continuously until modern times. Architects who were not trained in the mediaeval way, to work with their hands on the material, but only to make designs and to supervise, were uncommon until the end of the eighteenth century.

We have already mentioned Master Robert at St. Albans abbey and the English William who was in charge at Canterbury. Other great architects were Adam Lock at Wells and Alexander at Lincoln; later in the thirteenth century Henry of Reyns worked for the king at Westminster Abbey. Later still Edward I employed many masters including Walter of Hereford who had built part of Winchcombe Abbey and then had charge at Caernarvon Castle. It was in the fourteenth century that individual ideas were provided by several great architects, each of whom was responsible for a different fashion. The rich form of window tracery called "Curvilinear" was developed by Ivo of Raghton, who designed the east window at Carlisle Cathedral and the west window at York Minster. The tall tower and spire at Salisbury were added by Richard Farleigh, who had a wide practice, working also at Bath and Reading. Thomas Witney was in charge at Winchester Cathedral and then at Exeter. William Ramsey, the inventor of the "Perpendicular" style, was at Norwich and then came to London to be the king's master mason. He was so famous that he was called in to Lichfield Cathedral, 120 miles from London, then a journey of four days or more each way.

Two very important carpenters designed great

Lichfield Cathedral, altered by William Ramsey, the King's mason, in 1337–49.

works at the same period. William Hurley, who was the king's carpenter, also went to Ely Cathedral to build the timber lantern that took the place of the stone Norman tower which fell in 1322. This amazingly ingenious piece of carpentry was a completely new idea and showed that it was possible to build a timber roof across a space, the new octagon, far wider than the longest beam. The same idea, but applied quite differently to a long chamber, was the new roof designed for Westminster Hall by Hugh Herland in 1394. This made it possible to get rid of the rows of great posts which had supported the roof of the Norman hall built for William Rufus three hundred years before. Herland had earlier designed timber roofs for the colleges of William of Wykeham at Oxford and Winchester, and his timber "fan vault" over Winchester College Chapel still survives.

The greatest master masons in the second half of the fourteenth century were both in the king's service: Henry Yeveley and William Wynford. Between them they succeeded in popularizing the Perpendicular style which had been introduced by their predecessor William Ramsey about 1330. Yeveley was the older man, and became prominent soon after the Black Death, the great plague of 1349. In London most of the artists and craftsmen died and for some years after 1350 there were fine opportunities for men from distant parts of the country. Yeveley came from Derbyshire and Wynford from Somerset. They met in London, but while Yeveley was in charge of the royal works in the capital, Wynford was architect at Windsor Castle. It was Wynford who also became architect to William of Wykeham, bishop of Winchester and prime minister. The rebuilding of the nave of Canterbury Cathedral and the extension of Westminster Abbey were done under Yeveley. Wynford, in addition to Wykeham's Colleges, also

The chapel of New College, Oxford (1380–86). The design of Hugh Herland's timber roof was followed in the restoration.

Winchester Cathedral:
the nave as designed by
William Wynford in
1394 to replace the
Norman work.

designed the new nave of Winchester Cathedral. This was ingeniously transformed by cutting away parts of the old Norman building and inserting new stones. Yeveley died in 1400, the same year as the poet Geoffrey Chaucer; Wynford and the carpenter Hugh Herland both died in 1405.

The Builders' Tools

In modern times we think of architects and engineers using instruments and the working craftsmen handling tools. In fact both instruments and tools are developments of the same basic equipment. Both for design and for shaping of pieces of material, the basic tools are the square and the compass. Some form of pencil or point to draw a line is also needed for use with the square. Design as proportional geometry is independent of measurement, but in practice it is also necessary to have rods and lines marked with units such as feet and inches. In the Middle Ages there were measuring rods of six feet and also the longer "rod, pole or perch" which had different lengths. Although the standard rod was $16\frac{1}{2}$ feet, there were also rods of 18 feet or 20 feet in some parts of the country. Houses, barns and other buildings were commonly built in bays one rod wide, and halls and churches were often two rods (33 feet as a standard) in span.

For making drawings on parchment or paper, pencils of lead and of red chalk were used, and also pens. The quill pen and the reed pen could be used for freehand drawing, but not for ruling fine lines, and during the Middle Ages the "ruling pen" was invented, of metal blades held by a screw which could be turned to make a wider or narrower line. None of these pens has yet been found, but their traces can be seen scored into the sheets on which they were employed. For a long time compasses were all what we now call dividers, with two sharp points. For that reason the curves on drawings were always lightly scratched and then inked in freehand with a quill. Compasses with a pencil or a ruling pen on one arm came much later.

The working tools used in building included various kinds of hammers and axes, chisels for cutting joints in wood and for carving, and cold chisels for stone, used with a hammer. Timber was cut into planks with saws, generally of the long type working in a pit with two sawyers, a "top sawyer" and a "bottom sawyer". To lay stones or bricks properly it was also essential to have a plumb-line for verticals and a level. The spirit level with a bubble inside a glass tube is a modern invention, and until the later nineteenth century plumb levels were used. These were of different kinds but in all of them the

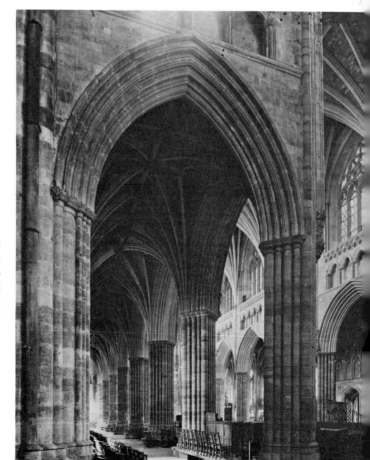

At Exeter Cathedral the nave was built in 1328–42 by Thomas Witney, an architect who had come from Winchester.

principle was the same. A triangular square, or a tee-square with the head much longer than the arm, had a short plumb line suspended from the apex of the triangle or the end of the stem. This hung in a slot so that when it hung straight, the base of the triangular square or cross-bar of the tee was level.

With this essentially simple apparatus, and the cranes and ram previously mentioned, the men of the Gothic age succeeded in their purpose. They built greater buildings, and more of them, than anyone else had ever done. After five hundred years of loss and destruction the remains of mediaeval civilization are still impressive. We have nothing to equal the great cathedrals, no modern house or palace can be compared with Westminster Hall. The spires of Salisbury, Lichfield and Norwich stand without serious rival. Yet the tale was not told: as we shall see, the Gothic tradition still had a long race to run.

Norwich Cathedral from the East: note the flying buttresses.

CHAPTER FOUR

Perpendicular to Renaissance

The Gothic style which had begun in France became the only kind of building in western Europe within a century. In spite of the differences of detail in different places, early Gothic was essentially international. Just as students from all parts flocked to the first universities in the twelfth century, so in the opposite direction architects and craftsmen spread outwards over Europe. All countries from Norway to Italy and from Portugal to Poland were infected, as it were, with the new idea. Except for Rome itself, it seemed that Roman architecture was over and done with, and with it the round arch and the heavy solidity of Roman and Romanesque walls and columns.

The pointed arch drew the eye upwards so that, instead of following the level lines of beams and cornices, it looked towards the sky. Tall towers, tall lancet windows, tall slender shafts, all gave emphasis in the same direction. As time went on this upward tendency became more marked. Not only were the individual parts of buildings arranged so as to point upwards: they appeared to grow away from the ground like plants. A typical tower would have a solid base, like the trunk of a tree, and as it rose the storeys of windows grew larger, letting in more and more light. At the top a pierced cresting or parapet gave the effect of leaves.

Inside the building the piers with their shafts, carrying upper stages of windows and the ribs of a vault branching out into space, conveyed the same impression of natural growth.

We cannot now be sure how far the designers intended that their work should have these meanings. Certainly they intended symbolism of the revealed truths of religion. Even before the Gothic style began, Honorius of Autun had written about 1130 that church buildings were set on a stone foundation as "the Church is founded on the sure rock of Christ." The earthly church building "rises on high between four walls, while the Church grows to a height of virtues through the four Gospels." The material stones of the church "are held together with mortar, as the faithful are linked by the bond of love." Clergy and architects together thought along these lines, but it is likely that the results were achieved subconsciously.

In being vertical instead of horizontal, Gothic style was the exact opposite of the earlier Romanesque way of building. But there was a great difficulty in getting away from the old ideas. The way a great church was built, from one end to the other, bit by bit as money came in, tended to make it look like a row of separate pieces. At first, even in Gothic times, each bay stood by itself. The tall lancet windows were at first used one by one. Gradually the designers came to feel that this was unsatisfactory and began to group windows together, in twos and threes. Later still the group of openings was placed under an arch which marked the group as a larger unit. Eventually the spaces at the top between the lancets and beneath the arch were pierced with patterns, and so tracery began. Inside the building the same sort of thing was happening to the vault. To begin with vaults had been solid surfaces, imitating the Roman vaults of concrete. Then came the idea of building arches or "ribs" first, and then filling in the spaces between them with quite thin stones like a shell. As the vaults were made larger and higher, more ribs were needed to make it possible for the shell to be built over the gaps between them. So as time went on the pattern of ribs became more and more complicated, and in many ways resembled the window tracery.

All through the early part of this development the main inventions came from the northern part of France. The architects of Paris and of the cathedrals at Sens, Chartres, Rheims and Amiens, of the abbey of St. Denis, and of many other great buildings, set the fashion. We cannot here follow all the details, but the biggest single step forward was the invention of "bar tracery" at Rheims Cathedral by its architect Jean d'Orbais, soon after 1210. All the later story of Gothic windows and details, not only in France but all over Europe, starts from the new ideas at Rheims. The reason why an idea could so quickly travel for hundreds of miles in an age without newspapers, telegraphs or even any official postal service, was that the people who mattered used the same language. In building, the people who mattered were the clients: kings, bishops and nobles; and their architects. The bishops and all the clergy spoke and wrote Latin; the kings and the courtiers all spoke French. Many of the architects, who had to work for both royal and clerical patrons, knew both languages. In England after the Norman Conquest, most of them spoke English too.

The Normans, who originally spoke a form of Danish, all used French by the time they conquered south Italy and then England in the middle of the eleventh century. The great armies of Crusaders who went out to Palestine were very largely French-speaking, so that French was the language of command. In England the children at school

were taught in French for more than two hundred
years (until 1350). If they went on to grammar
school (where grammar meant Latin grammar)
they were taught in Latin, and to speak Latin to
one another. Compared to the whole population,
the number who learned both French and Latin
might be small; but because they were not very
many it was possible to keep in touch with each
other. Just as scientists in one specialized subject
manage to keep in touch across the world today,
so the few great architects in the Middle Ages got
to know each other, and to hear of new inventions.

This was made still easier by the organization
of the master masons. Probably based upon the
guilds of later Roman times, this organization was
able to cross frontiers and bring together masters
in consultation over some difficult job. We know
of many instances of this spread over several
centuries. Lombard masters from North Italy went
to France and Spain; French masters like William
of Sens came to England or went to Sweden and
Sicily; German as well as French architects were
consulted at the building of Milan Cathedral. For
a long time, until about 1300, this internationalism
meant that in spite of local differences, Gothic
developed in the same way almost everywhere.
Things began to change during the fourteenth
century. Rivalry between kings as persons led to
dependence on the selfish interests of nations and
classes, set against one another. The fact that
Edward III of England had a genuine dynastic
claim to the throne of France led to centuries of
national conflict. New ideas of nationalism gained
strength in Flanders, where Edward was recognized as overlord. England tended to become allied
with Spain and with Germany against France.
It was this complicated political background in
the middle of the fourteenth century that led to
the Gothic way of building being split apart.

We cannot follow the parts of the story that lie overseas, but the rise of national feeling in England helped to produce a national style in architecture. This was in many ways quite unlike earlier Gothic and it was particularly unlike the French Gothic being built at the same time. As has been said, this new "Perpendicular" style was invented about 1330 by the master mason William Ramsey. At the time it began, this was only one of a number of personal fashions started by important architects in different parts of England. But because in 1336 Ramsey was appointed king's mason to Edward III, it was his fashion that won. What was accepted at the king's court soon became the rule over the whole country. The strangest thing about this development is that the slightly earlier fashion of richly flowing lines, called "Curvilinear", which had been developed by Ivo of Raghton in the North of England, was so greatly admired abroad that it became the source of later French and German style.

The two fashions were completely unlike one another, but they both set out to achieve the same object. The earlier Gothic, for all its clear beauty, had lacked unity. In spite of the invention of bar tracery, the old Romanesque ideas of building up bit by bit still affected design. By the late thirteenth century this was realized by the leading masters, and the new fashions were efforts to bring the parts of a building together. The flowing curve produced by joining together two arcs struck with compasses from opposite directions, and called the "ogee", was the basis of Curvilinear. Instead of tracery patterns being formed of separate circles, trefoils and quatrefoils which touched one another, the ogee curve linked all parts of the design together. A special form of this pattern was the "Reticulated" or netlike, where the main lines wandered to and fro, continually reversing until

63

the space was filled.

The beginning of the Perpendicular idea came from the Reticulated, but instead of each link in the mesh being made up of flowing curves, it was as if it had been pulled straight, like the mesh of wire netting. The main straight lines ran up and down and emphasized the vertical. This was what Gothic had always done, so the new idea was in harmony with the style. At the same time there was another tendency which had a great deal to do with the formation of a fresh style. This was the increase in size of windows.

Windows in the Dark Ages had appropriately been very small. They were points of danger in savage times. Houses, churches and monasteries, as well as castles, were built to keep enemies out. This idea was still in charge through the Romanesque period of our Norman architecture. But the strong government of the Norman kings, and later of Henry II, led to a different and more peaceful way of life. It was no longer necessary to fear marauding bands when law and order, the King's Peace, spread steadily over the land. In the changed circumstances there was no need to creep around in the dark or to waste torches and candles in daytime. It was common sense to let in more light. At the same time, this could in churches be regarded as symbolic as well. God as the Light of the World brightened the minds of men, and this could be symbolized in church by the light of the Sun shining through the windows of brightly coloured glass. The stained glass itself became brighter and more white glass was used as a background. Instead of the "dim religious light" of earlier times, all was brilliance.

The increase in size of windows meant a new risk, that the glass might be blown in by a gale. To prevent this it was necessary to make the stone bars of the window stronger. This could be done by building in an iron bar across the window and passing it through the vertical mullions. It was still stronger if the crossbar was made of stone; this was called a transom. The vertical mullions could be stronger still if they went straight from the sill of the window up to the arch. It was this last idea that became the main motive of Perpendicular. All large windows, divided by mullions into several lights, were thus united from top to bottom. They were also linked from side to side by one or more stone transoms. In principle the whole arrangement formed a gridiron, and that is what some of the later windows looked like.

Besides strength there was another great advantage in windows of this kind. The open sections or panels into which they were divided by the mullions and transoms were ideal in shape and size to hold stained glass figures of saints and personages of Bible history. In the same way, the tracery openings with straight vertical sides were simpler to fill with suitable designs than the Curvilinear spaces which curved in all directions and had no straight lines at all. Furthermore, the methods of setting out for the stones were also much simplified. The pieces for Perpendicular tracery could be cut far more easily than the twisted sections of a Curvilinear window. Consequently the work cost less and at least part of it could be done by men who were less highly skilled. After the great plague of 1349, when skilled men were hard to find, this gave the new style a great economic advantage.

This does not mean that there was anything cheap and shoddy about Perpendicular buildings. On the whole they were well built and the masons of the time took advantage of the great store of knowledge that had been built up in the previous two or three hundred years. The architects went on experimenting, so that right on to the end of the Middle Ages the ingenuity of the designers and the quality of their work continued to improve. This can be seen particularly in the towers and vaults built in the fifteenth and early sixteenth centuries. This period of splendid activity was still in full swing when it was cut short by the dissolution of the monasteries and chantries and the changed religious outlook of the Reformation.

In the same period that all this was happening in England, quite a different movement began in Italy. In and around Rome the influence of the remains of the old round-arched Roman buildings had always been too strong for the Gothic style to take root. The poet Petrarch pleaded for the preservation of Roman ruins and from the middle of the fourteenth century there was a steadily increasing interest in Roman art and in Latin literature. This movement was the Renaissance, and in the end it came to affect the whole world in some way. At first it was just the local counterpart of the nationalism that in northern Europe was producing separate Gothic styles such as Perpendicular. It is important, however, to distinguish between the aims and results of the two movements. The Romans of the time (quite rightly) believed themselves to be inferior to the ancient Romans. They therefore thought that they should improve themselves by imitating ancient art and literature. The Gothic artists, from early in the twelfth century, and on until the sixteenth, were quite sure that they knew better than the men of earlier times. They never looked backward for old forms to copy, but always pressed ahead to find fresh worlds to conquer.

Progress did not, of course, go on at a uniform pace. Changes in artistic fashion were geared to the personality of kings, bishops and noblemen. The quality of work was affected by the political background and by economic depression or prosperity. Periods of war and general destruction, when vast sums of money were spent on offence and defence, were not favourable to fine building. Revolution and civil war, which beset England from 1399 until 1461, meant a breakdown of law and order. In such conditions it is surprising that so much of importance did get built. But in contrast we can see that far more was achieved in the next two generations, from about 1475 to 1535.

The great triumphs of early Perpendicular had been the transformation of Westminster Hall, the rebuilding of the naves of Canterbury and Winchester cathedrals, and Wykeham's two colleges. After the dynastic revolution of 1399 and the deaths of the great architects Yeveley, Herland and Wynford within the next few years, there was a long period of slump. Subsidies to architecture were again given by Henry V, and his son Henry VI grew up to be one of England's greatest patrons of architecture. Eton College and King's College Chapel at Cambridge, though left unfinished when the king was murdered in 1471, gave great opportunities to the two royal architects Robert Westerley and Reginald Ely. In both cases there was complete planning and design from the start.

From the time of Yeveley and Wynford onwards, English architects had been improving the courtyard plan. This had started long before with the arrangement of monastic buildings around a square cloister. The same idea was applied to castles, to colleges, and to mansions and manorhouses. In some cases there was only one courtyard, in others two or more, but the buildings were never built haphazard as they had been until 1300 or later. The idea of unity and of each part contributing to the whole, had taken the place of adding bit by bit. The application of the same plan form to different types of building tended to give unity to architecture as a whole, not just to each single

Westminster Hall roof (1394–1400) has a span of 68 feet. It was designed for Richard II by Hugh Herland to replace Norman posts.

building.

Within the fifteenth century four main fashions in architecture followed each other. The first was really negative: a pause during the depression that followed the revolution of 1399. Little money was available for large works and there was a rather lifeless continuation of the style and methods of the end of the fourteenth century. After the accession of Henry V in 1413 there was a period of relative prosperity. There were no architects of genius, but the surviving pupils of Yeveley and Wynford tried to enrich their buildings with a good deal of repetitive decoration. The forms of Perpendicular tracery were continued as panelling on wall surfaces. Mouldings became smaller and detail rather fussy and complicated. By 1440 there was a reaction against this and influential persons had the detail of the Oxford Divinity Schools simplified. It may be that economy in cost was in part the reason for this, but it seems that King Henry VI agreed in disapproval of fussy details.

The design of the Divinity School at Oxford, built in 1423–80, was simplified after criticism by 'magnates of the realm.'

For in 1448 he set out his scheme for King's College, Cambridge, and particularly declared that the work should be "of large form, clean and substantial" and that it should avoid "superfluity of too great curious works of carving and busy moulding."

This puritanical reaction against elaboration lasted for a generation, until well after Edward IV had won the throne. The next great change came after his short exile in Flanders in 1470–71. After his return it is evident that the king was keen to imitate the richness of the buildings and decoration he had seen abroad. He began to lavish money on public buildings and on Windsor Castle, and his lead was followed. The rich late Gothic style generally known as Tudor was, historically, Yorkist, but it became famous as the style of the two first kings of the Tudor dynasty, Henry VII and Henry VIII. To this period of lavish enrichment belong many of the larger parish churches scattered over England, St. George's Chapel in Windsor Castle, Bath Abbey, the great tower of Canterbury Cathedral, the vaults (and much else) of King's College Chapel and, above all, the fantastic Henry VII's Chapel at Westminster.

In the earlier years of Henry VIII it would have seemed impossible that all this would within a few years be cut short. Quite suddenly everything began to happen at once. Decoration imitated from ancient Roman buildings spread from Italy to France and so, as a matter of the latest royal fashion, was taken up by Henry VIII. The Church was attacked by the Reformers and lost support. Lavish spending beyond the nation's means meant what we should now call an unbalanced budget. Finally, Henry VIII's personal difficulties over obtaining a divorce led to his repudiation of the Pope. A few years later the monasteries were dissolved and yielded immense sums which put the

King's College Chapel at Cambridge, completed in 1508–15 in a rich style which disregarded Henry VII's desire for simple detail.

exchequer on its feet again and enabled the king to build coastal defences against the French.

Once Henry VIII was dead (1547) the government ruling in the name of the boy king, Edward VI, became extremely Protestant. All chantries (to pray for souls) were abolished, and most colleges and hospitals except for a few which could show that they had been founded for education or for pure charity and not for purposes now considered superstitious. The new ruling class was composed of men who had been able to buy the lands that had belonged to the monasteries. So within a few years the national way of life was entirely changed. Instead of buildings being very largely churches and chapels (for chantry priests), they became almost entirely great houses. The new ruling class had the money to build; it was in possession of many dismantled monasteries. In many cases the answer was the obvious one: an old abbey became a new mansion. Elsewhere the old materials were taken down and used to build a new house in another place.

The style in which the new houses were built was, to begin with, the same Tudor form of Perpendicular, though with some of the newly fashionable decoration based on Roman sources. But very soon there was a deliberate attempt to avoid Gothic style and to substitute an imitation of Roman architecture. This began at the top. Edward VI's uncle the Duke of Somerset became Lord Protector and decided to build himself a private palace in London. On the site of the town house of the bishops of Worcester, pulled down in 1549, he had built the first Renaissance building in England. Even though it took a very long time for imitation of classical Roman style to become the rule, the first step had been taken by the middle of the sixteenth century, with the building of old Somerset House.

The sudden and complete change in fashion has to be explained. Three different causes all contributed to make the artistic revolution possible. First of all there was the destruction, not merely of the monasteries, but of the power of the Church. The greatest of the patrons of the Gothic architects no longer existed. There were no continuing jobs of the old kind, for even at the cathedrals which survived, building work stopped for two hundred years or more. Secondly, the fashion at the royal court for decorations in the imitative classical style put Gothic details out of favour. Foreign artists, mostly not architects at all, could draw the fashionable "antique" work on paper and get better pay than master masons. Finally, the books of Vitruvius had appeared in print. Anyone who could read, and learned to draw, was able to make designs of his own in the Roman manner.

The geometrical rules for designing Gothic buildings were very complicated. To be a sound Gothic architect meant spending an apprenticeship of seven years learning how to cut stone, to set it properly, and to carve it. On top of that another three years at least were demanded before the methods of proportion and design could be mastered. The body of tradition which had grown

Herstmonceux Castle, begun in 1441 and restored in 1913–35, now houses the new Greenwich Observatory.

up in over four hundred years, though still alive, was a large and heavy subject to study. To make it worth while there had to be good jobs at the end. Now, by 1550, these jobs had stopped. So the way was open to the amateurs, including some of the new nobility and gentry, who wished to show off as men of taste. Armed with a copy of Vitruvius, or with one of the new pattern books which began to be produced, they set to work to design buildings on paper.

The actual building still had to be done by craftsmen who knew how to handle materials and could make the house stand up. But they were controlled by the new amateur architects. For nearly four centuries England suffered—and still suffers—from this division. Whereas all Romanesque and Gothic buildings, and indeed most ancient Greek and Roman buildings, were designed by the same men who knew all about putting them up, architects since the Renaissance have designed on paper without personal knowledge of how it was to be built. Architects more and more became "professional men" remote from the master craftsmen who had building skills.

Fortunately this did not all happen at once. Until the beginning of the nineteenth century a very large number of houses and even some churches and public buildings were designed by mason-architects, bricklayer-architects and joiner-architects. Only a few of them were able to reach the top and be accepted as professional men in their own right. One of the last was John Carr (1723–1807), who trained under his father, a Yorkshire master mason himself.

The first hundred years of the English Renaissance produced the great Elizabethan and Jacobean mansions. Some of these were traditional houses with some classical trimmings added; a few were serious attempts to produce architecture in the Roman manner. New ideas of comfort and convenience meant that the houses of ordinary men and women began to be larger and better built. Brickwork came to be used more and more as a stronger and more fireproof form of construction. It was also much cheaper.

A few large buildings were still put up by highly competent masters of the old style. Such was Wadham College at Oxford, built in 1610–1613 by masons from Somerset, working under William Arnold. In timber building the great carpenter John Abel of Herefordshire was an architect and designed and built market halls and other important works during a life of 97 years (1577–1674), but mostly from 1613 to 1654. Much of the old tradition survived through the works of such craftsmen. Remains of the style, the "Gothic Survival," went on for another hundred years. But to become recognized and earn high fees it became essential to study Vitruvius, or copy books of plates mostly produced on the Continent. The national style of England slowly disappeared.

The great western Gatehouse of Hampton Court Palace, built for Cardinal Wolsey in 1515–25 by Henry Redman; later given to Henry VIII.

CHAPTER FIVE

Reviving Old Styles

In the sixteenth century, when the traditional style of building began to give way to the Renaissance, another great change was taking place. A very large number of ordinary houses were pulled down and rebuilt, and many others were built on new sites. This process had begun earlier in some places, for in the twenty years or so that Sir John Fastolf was lord of the manor of Castle Combe in Wiltshire (he died in 1459), William Worcestre recorded that some fifty houses were rebuilt, newly built, or in two cases were repaired. Five at least of the new houses were built of stone. More than a hundred years later William Harrison described the condition of English housing as it was about 1585. He pointed out that most houses in England "except here and there in the west-country towns" were still of timber, the exceptions (including places like Castle Combe) being of stone. Harrison also quoted the Spaniards in England in the time when Queen Mary Tudor was married to King Philip. They were astonished that food was so plentiful in a country of poor housing: "These English have their houses made of sticks and dirt, but they fare commonly so well as the king."

Old men in Harrison's village could remember the time (presumably about 1525) when in most country villages there were not more than two or three chimneys apart from those in the great houses and monasteries. By the 1580's a multitude of chimneys had recently been built. The house was changing from a place to spend the night in into a real home. Chimneys to carry away the smoke from the fire cleared the air. Sheets of horn began to be put in the windows instead of linen or paper, and it was not long before glass in small leaded panes took the place of horn. It soon became possible to live and work inside the house, and this meant that many homes became small factories. Weaving and lacemaking were common home trades, but there were many others.

Ordinary people were beginning to spend much more money on their houses, and a certain degree of comfort came to be regarded as a necessity and not as a luxury. This brought with it the other side of the Spaniard's remark: Englishmen ran into debt for their improved houses and had less to spend on their food. Many of them, mortgaging the property to rebuild or improve the house, lost it a few years later because they could not pay off the mortgage. So the improved building of around 1600 was not by any means an unmixed blessing. Blessing or no, it had come to stay, and further luxuries were added as time went on. Very few houses or cottages exist today in anything like their original state. Every generation has added and altered, and careful restoration to the condition in which the house was built results in a discomfort which nobody would now tolerate.

Even apart from the alterations, not very many towns or villages have many buildings older than Elizabethan times. The few older houses, now regarded as small cottages, were probably quite substantial farmhouses when they were built. Those of 1500 or earlier generally had a hall open to the roof, with the smoke of an open hearth given plenty of space. At one or both ends would be rooms built in two storeys, one above another. In the small house which had only a hall and one wing, the single upper room would be the bedroom, and the ground floor room beneath it the only "best room." The open hall, generally smoky, served as kitchen, dining room and for all general purposes.

There was, of course, much more space and far more real comfort in the great houses, but even there it was hard to find privacy. As time went on sleeping chambers on the dormitory principle were divided by partitions to make separate bedrooms, but usually they opened out of each other. It was not common for space to be wasted on corridors, and money on separate doors, until quite a late date. For most people the sort of house that we now think of as a home did not begin to exist until early in the nineteenth century. The general installation of water closets and bathrooms is still in progress at this present time. From this we can see that it may take two hundred years for a change at the luxury level of society to reach everybody.

Change, relentless but irregular, was going on in this way, quite regardless of the changes in appearance. Architectural style was changing too, but the two sets of alterations had little to do with one another. What did happen was that changes of the practical kind were demanded of architects when they planned new houses. So they had to satisfy at the same time the fashion, so far as style was concerned, and also supply the normal comfort and convenience. Landlords who had rows of houses built as "rents," however, were only considering the scarcity value of accommodation. Some of these speculative ventures were squeezed into narrow spaces on town plots and were not well built. This brought in another factor which had not been common earlier:

building houses simply as a way of making money —not by the craftsmen for a particular client, but as a speculation on his own account or for a middleman. The origins of this practice have to be sought in the methods of monastic houses and parish and chantry trusts in the Middle Ages. To some extent, though seldom for private gain, the building of houses for letting had always been a form of investment.

There was not much change in the technical methods of building. The use of brick spread from the eastern side of England over most of the country, and a tax on bricks (by number) led to the use of very large thick bricks instead of thin ones. In stone masonry and timberwork the skills of the mediaeval period continued with little alteration or improvement. Probably the biggest difference was in the kinds of trusses used for roofs, because various copybooks on carpentry had been printed from the sixteenth century onwards. Among these was a famous and influential treatise by the French architect Philibert De l'Orme, published in 1561. Much later came the English book on craftsmanship generally, *Mechanick Exercises* (1678) by Joseph Moxon, an amateur scientist. One of the biggest changes was the extensive use of iron straps and nails to make strong joints, instead of wooden pegs.

The appearance of buildings changed a great deal. To some extent this was due to changes in the proportions of different materials used: the expansion of brick, the decline in timbering. There were also changing fashions in windows and window frames which altered the look of houses very greatly. When glass first became common in the windows of small houses, early in the seventeenth century, it was fixed with "cames" of lead directly onto a wooden frame, but onto an iron frame with hinges for the opening casements.

Later in the century, especially in the Commonwealth period, a much larger window became common, with a heavy frame of wood including a crosspiece or transom with two square lights above it. Opening casements were fitted beneath the transom. At the end of the century the double-hung sash window, sliding up and down in two pieces, came in and remained in fashion for 150 years. For much of the present century it has been in fashion again for "neo-Georgian" houses. For about sixty years the wooden glazing bars of sashes were heavy and thick, but in the later eighteenth century they became very slender. Even in earlier houses the late type of sash with thin glazing bars has generally been substituted, except perhaps in the windows of the attics and basement.

We can now consider what happened in architectural style from the Renaissance to our own century. First of all came the long period, already mentioned, in which buildings were still essentially Gothic. The forms of Roman art, or at least, what were believed to be Roman forms, were applied as a decoration. The look of the buildings changed a good deal, but under the surface they remained very much the same. The earliest Roman details were supplied by Italian artists who visited the courts of Henry VII and Henry VIII. Then came second-hand versions through France. In the later sixteenth century the main influences were from Holland and North Germany and moved away from really Roman forms to a very ugly style that seems mainly to have been invented by engravers of title pages for books.

After 1600 there was a good deal of influence from Holland, but it was very largely in brickwork and affected small houses rather than mansions or public buildings. A real architectural style at the top was again produced by Inigo Jones. Jones was

The west front of Montacute House in Somerset, an exceptionally fine and complete Elizabethan mansion of 1580–99.

a draughtsman and painter who took up the study of architecture and travelled in Italy. He there studied the books of Andrea Palladio, published in 1570, and later brought back Palladio's idea of style to England. Inigo Jones's most important works in this style were the Queen's House at Greenwich, begun in 1616, and the Banqueting Hall in Whitehall, started three years later. He also built the Chapel of Lincoln's Inn (1618–23) in a genuinely Gothic style, which he must have studied carefully. Jones and his relative and pupil John Webb were the two great architects of the first English "Palladianism".

The Restoration of Charles II in 1660 brought about a great change in all the arts. During his exile the king had come into close touch with the French court, and admired what was happening under his cousin Louis XIV. It became fashionable to look to France for leadership in style, and in France this style was set largely by Italians. They were far too up-to-date to be interested in the version of Roman architecture recorded and developed by Palladio. Their style had moved on and become what is called "Baroque"—rich and fantastic in comparison with the heavy monuments of ancient Rome. Although in England there was no real Baroque architecture, a good

The Queen's House at Greenwich, designed in the Palladian style by Inigo Jones in 1616, and finished for Henrietta Maria in 1635.

Wren's church of St Stephen Walbrook (1672–79) in London. After the Great Fire of 1666 Wren designed most of the new churches.

Vanbrugh, soldier and playright, designed Castle Howard in Yorkshire, an unusual example of English Baroque (1699–1706).

deal of the same spirit animated the designs of Sir Christopher Wren and of several of his followers. We all know how Wren, almost alone, designed all the new churches and public buildings needed to rebuild London after the Great Fire of 1666. The English architect who came nearest to adopting a truly Baroque style was Thomas Archer, whose greatest work was Birmingham Cathedral (St. Philip's), built in 1710–1725.

Before Wren was dead there had been a campaign against him and his style, and this was connected with the political upheaval of 1714, when Queen Anne died. The replacement of the Stuarts by the Hanoverian dynasty directly caused the reversion to a second Palladianism. This became the fashionable style of the Early Georgian period, lasting through the reigns of George I and George II. After this came another period of foreign influences, one after the other, but due to the studies of British architects abroad. Sir William Chambers tried to introduce a Chinese style (the pagoda in Kew Gardens); the brothers Adam copied the decorations that had been

The interior of Chiswick House, Lord Burlington's neo-Palladian villa of 1725.

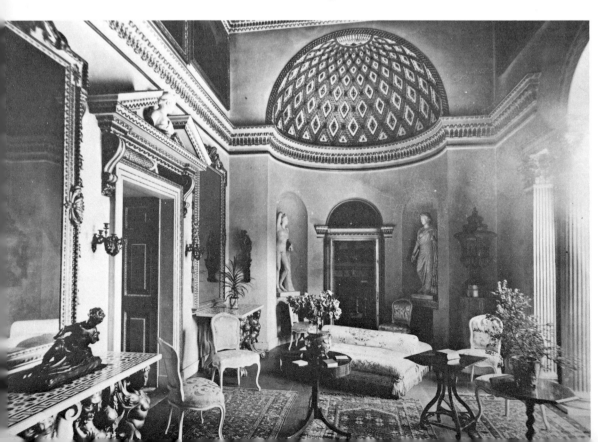

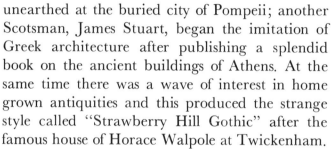

Prior Park (1735–48) (*above*) and the Circus (1754) (*right*) at Bath show the simple lines of the second Palladian period as understood by the architect John Wood.

Below. The pagoda (1761–62) in Kew Gardens, an attempt by Sir William Chambers to transplant the Chinese style.

unearthed at the buried city of Pompeii; another Scotsman, James Stuart, began the imitation of Greek architecture after publishing a splendid book on the ancient buildings of Athens. At the same time there was a wave of interest in home grown antiquities and this produced the strange style called "Strawberry Hill Gothic" after the famous house of Horace Walpole at Twickenham.

Serious interest in genuine Gothic buildings was aroused and towards the end of the eighteenth century they began to be studied carefully. Correct drawings of mediaeval work began to be made, by John Carter and others, and before 1800 a movement to save mediaeval buildings from destruction had started. For more than a generation this had very little effect on the design of new houses, churches or public buildings. The work done continued to be Late Georgian in one of its variants, as carried out by several famous architects. After about 1810, when the Prince of Wales became Regent for his father, the fashion changed into something less stiff and a great many buildings were faced with stucco, a hard plaster. Very often the term "Regency Style" is used to cover the period from soon after 1800 to the beginning of Queen Victoria's reign in 1837. In this period there were borrowings from Oriental architecture

The exterior of Brighton Pavilion, as altered in 1815–21 by John Nash, was deliberately 'Indian'.

The inside of the Pavilion is preserved as it was in the days when the Prince Regent was in residence.

(as at the Brighton Pavilion), from ancient Greece and Egypt, and from various mediaeval styles especially the Tudor.

Except for the great rebuilding of London churches by Wren and his successors, most building from 1550 to 1800 consisted of houses, great and small. There were a few public buildings, for example the new Somerset House of 1776–86, designed by Chambers. After 1800 public works and street architecture, such as the new Regent Street and Regent's Park terraces by John Nash, came to be far more important. At the same time a large share in building was taken by engineers, who came to be responsible for the design of bridges in particular. John Rennie, the designer of the old Waterloo Bridge (1810–17), and Thomas Telford, were the most famous of these engineers. Both of them were Scotsmen; Rennie trained with a millwright, but Telford served an apprenticeship with a mason and was in a special sense a link with traditional methods of the past, and the science of the future (as in his notable suspension bridges at Conway and over the Menai Straits).

Great factories and warehouses were being built as a result of the Industrial Revolution and the coming of steam power. For a long time these

Horace Walpole's Strawberry Hill (1747–76) at Twickenham gave its name to a neo-Gothic architectural style.

were built as cheaply as possible and without any concern for their surroundings. Some of the later buildings sought and achieved distinction in functional design. Among these is the outstanding yarn mill (now Messrs. Jarrolds' Works) at Norwich, built in sections from 1834 to 1840. The first part was designed by John Brown, the county surveyor of Norfolk, the architect for a good many churches and public buildings. The building is, therefore, not an outcome of vernacular tradition but a work of architecture and a fine one at that. It was one of the earliest, and most successful, of the attempts to give aesthetic quality to buildings purely utilitarian in purpose.

We cannot here consider the main body of engineering works produced by the Industrial Age. They provided, however, a completely new background to the subject of building in Britain. From the building of the Roman roads, starting in the first century, there had been no general attempt at a new national transport system until the canals. At first local, the inland waterways had become a linked system by 1790. They were overtaken by the similarly linked system of main-line railways less than sixty years later. The waterways, and still more steam railways, made it possible to move people and industrial products all over the country. In the course of another century or so this was to mean that most local and regional traditions died out.

Strangely enough, the new wave of uniform style spread over the country was first seen in the building of churches. Starting with the reign of Victoria or within a few years after 1837, there was a great religious revival. It was held that the cause of the Church could best be advanced by building many new churches in all districts, and by restoring or rebuilding the old churches. It was thought that the right model for the Church,

Conway Suspension Bridge, of 1824–26, was also by Telford.

The Menai Bridge to Anglesey, built by Thomas Telford in 1819–26.

in its architecture as in everything else, was to be found in the ways of the Middle Ages. The result was the Gothic Revival. Just as at the Renaissance, the men of the nineteenth century felt that they were inferior to their predecessors of long ago. Instead of the ruins of Rome it was now the ruined abbeys or the remains of churches and houses of the thirteenth and fourteenth centuries that were to be copied. Almost all British architects spent much time in drawing and studying these mediaeval buildings.

Everyone knows the name of Sir George Gilbert Scott, the most famous of the architects of the Gothic Revival. He restored many of the old cathedrals and built or rebuilt hundreds of churches. Towards the end of his life he designed the Midland Grand Hotel (1865–74) for St. Pancras Station in London, probably the most extraordinary of all the buildings produced in the course of the Revival. (Scott had nothing to do with St. Pancras Station itself, with its splendid pointed arched roof, the work of the engineer William Barlow). Besides Scott there were many other "Gothic Revival" architects, starting with A. W. N. Pugin and including William Butterfield

and George Edmund Street. The movement went on until the end of the nineteenth century and beyond. Liverpool (Anglican) Cathedral, designed by Sir Giles Gilbert Scott (grandson of Sir George), and begun in 1903, is the last great work of the Revival.

By no means all buildings of the time were in "Gothic" style, and it was not popular with everybody. Classical and Renaissance buildings were still admired, and in 1860 Scott himself was forced to use a Renaissance style for the new Government Offices in Whitehall. Club-houses, banks and most public buildings were based on Roman or Italian models, though Street's Law Courts (the Royal Courts of Justice, 1874–82) was a last attempt to show that Gothic was a style for all purposes. As time went on, architects studied mediaeval buildings over a wider area of Europe, and also gained a better knowledge of the Middle Ages. Yet none of them really succeeded in convincing the public, and by 1890 the arts were moving away in new directions. Alongside "Art Nouveau," the new art surprisingly influenced by Japan (though seldom showing the fact), there was one serious attempt at a new revival, of Byzantine architecture. Of this the finest example is the Roman Catholic Cathedral at Westminster, begun in 1895, designed by John Bentley.

Since the end of genuine Gothic there has been no single tradition in architectural design. The old traditions in vernacular building went on, and with only a slight influence from fashionable styles, lasted into the nineteenth century. Villages and country cottages, built and rebuilt by generation after generation of local craftsmen, carried on a part of the legacy left by the Middle Ages. The end really came with the founding of the Royal Institute of British Architects in 1834.

York Railway Station of 1867–77, by Thomas Prosser, is the best example of the great period of railway building.

The Midland Hotel at St Pancras (the station is in the background), shows the Gothic Revival at its most ornate in 1865–74.

From that time onwards the design of buildings became the preserve of a professional class, entirely separated from the practical knowledge of the master craftsmen of the building trades. Some part of the old traditions passed to the engineers who, unlike architects, had to spend a part of their training "in the shops". For this reason we may call St. Pancras Station, designed by an engineer, a real building. Its neighbour, Scott's great Hotel, is merely a work of architecture.

Westminster Cathedral (1895–1903), designed by John Bentley in the revived Byzantine style of the end of the last century.

CHAPTER SIX

And Now . . .

In the course of this short account of building
we have already come a long way. Taking the
world as a whole the story of architecture has
lasted for 2500 years, without counting the still
earlier remains of the great temples of Egypt. In
Britain, where there was little or no connection
between the work of the Romans and of the
Anglo-Saxons, we can at any rate look at a stream
of buildings spread over a thousand years. Starting
as a trickle of crude imitations of late Roman
building, the stream grew into a great river as
time went on. Flourishing styles and improved
methods of construction reached us from overseas.
The Normans brought with them the Romanesque, which had reached northern France from
Italy. Fifty years later, returning Crusaders who
had seen the effect of pointed arches were to start
the fashion which became Gothic. Out of the
Near East, the earliest home of great buildings,
came the elements of what was to be the one great
European style. At the very same time the pointed
arch, with much of the same knowledge of constructional skills, was the leading feature of
eastern Saracenic architecture. Gothic art in the
West, Egyptian, Persian and Turkish art in the
East, ran parallel courses through much the same
period.

The Guildhall (1448–60) at York, with its traditional wooden pillars.

Essentially both Gothic and Saracenic were styles based upon cut stone. In both cases their noblest buildings were covered with vaults or domes of stone or brick. It was for the most part only in secondary works that they were prepared to accept wooden roofs of beamed construction. In this respect Britain was a partial exception. So strong was the tradition of timber building in the North-West that wooden trusses were designed to span the king's hall at Westminster, the Guildhalls of London and York, and imitation vaults of wood were built over some great cathedrals. We can, because of this, see a good deal of the best of both worlds in this country. Certainly there is no other timber building in the world to be compared with Westminster Hall roof. On the other hand, at the end of the Gothic age, no other country can show a stone vault of equivalent skill and beauty to that of Henry VII's Chapel. This is not a matter for self-satisfaction or complacency, but is something to set against the fact that Britain in the Middle Ages was not one of the rich countries of Europe.

In prehistoric and Roman times Britain had been a corn growing country. In the Middle Ages it became to an increasing extent a place of sheep pastures. The sheep were kept mainly for their wool, which was exported abroad. As everyone knows, the Lord Chancellor in the House of Lords still sits on the Woolsack—a cushion actually stuffed with wool—as a symbol of the chief riches of the country. From the latter part of the fourteenth century there was a great deal of spinning and weaving of wool done in many parts of Britain, and this greatly increased local wealth. This is the main reason why in the districts of the "clothiers" (then the men who made cloth, not those who turned it into clothes) there were many fine churches and manor-houses built between 1375 and 1525. The two richest centres were East

Anglia (Norfolk and Suffolk) and Somerset, and that is why so many churches in those counties have splendid towers in the Perpendicular style, and carved wooden roofs borne up on angels.

After the Middle Ages came the period of colonial expansion, when explorers set out to find and bring back riches from East and West, and were followed by emigrants seeking cheaper land or greater freedom. At home the riches went largely to build the great mansions and to enable their owners to plant gardens, parks and avenues. It was this special feature of British homes from the seventeenth to the nineteenth century that has made the typical landscape, so unlike that of most other countries. As we have seen in regard to comfort and convenience in the house, the fashion set at the top gradually spread. By the end of the nineteenth century, all classes of the population were beginning to set their hopes on a home of their own with at least a small garden. It was this ambition that, to a large extent, accounted for the rapid spread of towns and cities.

While all this was happening, the developments in commerce and industry were causing even deeper changes. Besides the need for many more shops, offices, warehouses and factories, there was a far larger demand for homes from a swiftly increasing population. Instead of increasing material prosperity enabling ambitions—such as a house with a garden—to be more easily fulfilled, the vastly greater numbers of people constantly made further demands on the available land. This is the great problem of Britain in our own time: how to provide even merely adequate homes for so many, without swallowing up all the land of a small country. It is basically the attempt to find an answer to this urgent problem that has produced a new kind of building.

As we saw, all traditional building was of one

or other of two main kinds: either of stone or brick laid piece by piece, or framed with lengths of timber. By either method it was possible to make houses of several storeys, as high as the inhabitants cared to climb the stairs. Inside some walled cities (such as old Edinburgh) the houses were built very tall even centuries ago, because of the great demand for land. Exactly the same thing happened in the limited area of the island on which New York is built. The reasons there were less the demand for homes than the very high value of land for business purposes. The result, from the last years of the nineteenth century onwards, has been the rise of the "skyscraper".

There is a fundamental difference between the modern skyscraper and the tallest usable buildings of earlier periods. Firstly, it is only possible to build economically to enormous heights by means of newly invented methods of construction. Secondly, the users can only get up and down the building by the use of lifts or elevators, mechanical or electrical. The lift in the modern sense came into use only after 1850, and the modern types of building construction have developed even more recently. The combined result, after little more than one century, has been a complete revolution. As the years pass, the traditional methods of building are used less and less. Their place is taken by completely fresh skills, invented in a different way.

We have seen that in Britain the methods used by the Romans died out, and were later replaced by fresh importations: from Rome, from France, from Constantinople and from the Near East. But though the degree of skill in building a church or house might vary very much, the methods them- selves were on the whole alike. Individual master craftsmen of an inventive turn could devise a new way of spanning a wider hall or building a higher vault. The way of building did not stand still, but it tended to change slowly, and the great changes in appearance were on the surface. Essentially a builder of three thousand years ago would be at home on an ordinary building site of the early years of the twentieth century. Within one lifetime all this has changed.

All the development of building skills through the centuries had come about by trial and error. An idea was tested by using it. If the house fell down, the idea would be abandoned or improved. Except by making models on a small scale, rather than building at once to full size, there was no way of finding out whether an idea would work. At every stage each new invention was a matter of practice. It was only after 1800 that mathematical and scientific theory began to provide a completely different approach. In future each problem would be tackled by means of calculation, combined with scientific tests of materials to prove their strength. Though occasional mistakes could still happen, it was possible for the first time in history to work out in advance the precise way in which a building or a machine would behave. To be proof against accidents, additional strength is always given by multiplying the theoretical answer by a "factor of safety".

Even in the fourteenth century additional strength had been given to stone buildings by inserting links of iron. As time went on the practice grew and, as we saw, iron bands were used after the end of the Middle Ages for making strong joints in timber roofs. At last, in 1778, a building was made of iron, the famous Iron Bridge at Coalbrookdale. From then on, iron and steel came to be used more and more as part of building construction. Metal joists and beams were used for floors. Later still, metal roof trusses were used instead of timber. From 1855, when

The first iron building was the Bridge at Coalbrookdale in Shropshire, built in 1778.

The Palm House (1845–57) at Kew Gardens, finest survivor of the Victorian glass buildings invented by the gardener Sir Joseph Paxton.

iron beams of "I" section began to be made, experiments in framed construction became possible. The forms of timber framing were found to be effective and, after about 1890, large buildings began to be erected with steel frames, and the panels filled in with brick or other substances.

The earlier skyscrapers were made possible by this development of steel construction, and the size of the supports could be settled by calculation. Many buildings still are made with steel frames, but after only a generation the invention of the steel framed structure was followed by the still more revolutionary reinforced concrete. Concrete itself had become possible in the modern sense only with the discovery of artificial (Portland) cement about 1825. Gradually this came to be combined in use with metal joists, and towards the end of the nineteenth century true "reinforced concrete" was invented in France. It was at first adopted only very slowly but became general as a result of forced economy in the use of steel during the First World War of 1914–18. Reinforced concrete has established itself during the last fifty years as an entirely new form of construction, quite unlike anything possible in earlier history.

The strength of concrete construction depends

partly upon great improvements in the quality of the cement used. Testing of materials and of models has led to better theoretical formulae. The precise positions where metal reinforcement should be placed have also been worked out by mathematical means. A fresh step was taken with the invention of "prestressed" concrete by the Frenchman Eugène Freysinnet in 1904. By substituting very strong steel rods or wires, already "pretensioned" (stretched), for ordinary metal reinforcing rods, much lighter and stronger construction could be achieved. It was not until after 1930 that the method came into general use and it was once again the need for economy of materials in the second World War that brought it into worldwide prominence. It is a method that calls for greater precision and a higher quality of craftsmanship than either steel framing or ordinary reinforced concrete construction. For these reasons it has still to be regarded as an experimental material about which there is still much to learn.

The long period of attempts to revive ancient styles of architecture, or to import fresh ideas from distant parts of the world (particularly Japan), ended soon after 1900. It was followed by a deep disillusionment which lasted for fifty years. The feeling that mere imitation of historical detail was an admission of defeat steadily grew along with the twentieth century. This led to the view that building should be entirely practical, made to serve a purpose and without any attempt at beauty. This view of architecture is called "Functionalism", on the ground that it fulfils a practical function and that if it does so well, it will automatically look right.

This functionalist theory, attractive as it sounds, did not work well in practice. Not only decoration or detail that imitated past styles was left out, but all decoration or enrichment. Every surface was

The front of Norwich City Hall, built in 1932–38 under the influence of the brick style of Northern Europe.

left flat and plain, without mouldings or any features (apart from door and window openings) to break the monotony. The modern functionalist buildings thus tended to have no light and shade but to appear as crude obtrusive blocks. This effect was made even worse by two other factors. The first of these was the deliberate neglect of proportion. It was held that any shape that happened to suit the practical purpose of the building must be a good shape. Secondly, colour and texture of surface were not regarded as important. Concrete made with Portland cement, just as it left the builders' hands, was accepted automatically because it was "functional".

Traditional architecture and methods were thrown out, but for a long time there was little sign that anything really worthy was to be put in their place. What little there was came mainly from two sources, of which one was traditional: the brick building of northern Europe. In Scandinavia, North Germany and Holland a series of important brick buildings, with many smaller ones, was built in the first thirty years of this century. The other really good buildings were designed, not by architects, but by engineers. Outstanding among the many new bridges were those of the Swiss engineer Robert Maillart, making use of the new material, reinforced concrete. Maillart, unlike the architects of his time, sought and achieved beauty as well as merely practical function. From his early works (notably the Rhine Bridge at Tavanasa of 1905) onwards, Maillart pointed the way towards the future.

The same direction was followed by other engineers, not only in building bridges, but in the design of concrete trusses or vaults for exhibition halls. For such purposes space and light, with economical structure, were essential. Very slowly, between the two World Wars and for some time after the second, this movement gathered strength. Not many of its achievements were outstanding, nor were many of them intended to last for more than a few years. None the less they provided a background for further experiment and development. Much of the most interesting work in recent years has been done in Italy, where Pier Luigi Nervi has shown that it is possible to use reinforced concrete to express concepts of beauty as well as material function. There are signs that his lead is being followed by other engineers, and there is a growing realization that beauty of form, colour and texture is just as worthwhile as fitness for some practical purpose.

Most of the serious developments in building of recent years have been outside Britain. This is not to say that we have not already profited from the use of new materials and methods. In a quiet way, for many smaller buildings, the introduction of laminated timber has been a constructional landmark. Lamination is a method of building up timbers of required sizes from thin layers glued together with special modern adhesives. The result is a strong, economical and effective material which in some sense returns to the great English tradition of timber frames and timber roofs. Modern reinforced plate glass, though an expensive material and used too much by some recent designers, is at times effective. Experiments in giving concrete a pleasing surface by the use of special kinds of stone and pebble and by "hammer dressing" are removing much of the objection to the appearance of modern work. Finally we may take pleasure in the outstanding works of modern engineering such as the Forth and Severn road bridges. If a third, planned to cross the Humber within a few years, is built, it will have the longest clear span ever achieved.

For Further Reading

The subjects of Architecture and Building are so large that reference must be made to specialized bibliographies. Among these are the current issues of READERS' GUIDE TO BOOKS ON ARCHITECTURE by the County Libraries Section of The Library Association; the Book List ARCHITECTURE of The National Book League; and the BASIC LIST OF BOOKS of the Royal Institute of British Architects. Attention is also drawn to the very great value of the ENGLISH LOCAL HISTORY HANDLIST (edited for the Historical Association by F. W. Kuhlicke and F. G. Emmison, 4th edition, 1969). The short list which follows is intended only to cover the general background.

Atkinson, T. D., *Local Style in English Architecture* (Batsford, 1947).

— —, *A Glossary of Terms used in English Architecture* (Methuen, revised edition, 1946).

Bond, F., *Gothic Architecture in England* (Batsford, 1906).

Briggs, M. S., *The Architect in History* (Oxford, Clarendon Press, 1927).

— —, *A Short History of the Building Crafts* (Oxford, Clarendon Press, 1925).

Brunskill, R. W., *Illustrated Handbook of Vernacular Architecture* (Faber, 1970).

Clifton-Taylor, A.· *The Pattern of English Building* (1962; revised edition, Faber, 1972).

Crossley, F. H. *Timber Building in England* (Batsford, 1951).

Davey, N. *A History of Building Materials* (Phoenix House, 1961).

Fletcher, Sir B. *History of Architecture on the Comparative Method* (revised edition, Athlone Press, 1961).

Harvey, J. *English Cathedrals* (Batsford, 1950; revised paperback edition, 1963).
English Mediaeval Architects—A Biographical Dictionary down to 1550 (Batsford, 1954).
The Gothic World 1100–1600 (Batsford, 1950; paperback edition, Harper Colophon, 1969).
The Cathedrals of Spain (Batsford, 1957).
The Master Builders (Thames & Hudson, 1971).
The Mediaeval Architect (Wayland, 1972).

Innocent, C. F. *The Development of English Building Construction* (1916; reprint, David & Charles, 1971).

Lethaby, W. R. *Architecture* (1911; revised edition, Oxford University Press, 1955).

Lloyd, N. *Illustrated History of English Brickwork* (H. G. Montgomery, 1925).

Pannell, J. P. M. *An Illustrated History of Civil Engineering* (Thames & Hudson, 1964).

Pelican History of Art (Penguin Books; volumes by various authors on periods and places).

Pevsner, N. *An Outline of European Architecture* (Penguin Books; revised paperback edition, 1963).

Plommer, H. *Ancient and Classical Architecture* (Longmans, Green, 1956).

Salzman, L. F. *Building in England down to 1540* (Oxford, Clarendon Press, 1952; revised edition, 1967).

Stewart, Cecil *Early Christian, Byzantine and Romanesque Architecture* (Longmans, Green, 1954).

Whiffen, M. *Stuart and Georgian Churches outside London, 1603–1837* (Batsford, 1948).

Wood, M. *The English Mediaeval House* (Phoenix House, 1965).

Date Chart

The date chart which follows gives a selection only of important buildings, from the founding of Rome to the present time. Many buildings are left out because their dates are not known. After AD 1100 special attention is given to British examples, including works in Scotland and Wales, which could not be individually mentioned in the text. In compiling this chart much use has been made of Fletcher's *History of Architecture* and of volumes in the *Pelican History of Art* (see Book List, pages 96–97); also of *Chinese Art* by William Willetts (Penguin Books, 1958) and of *A History of Ottoman Architecture* by Godfrey Goodwin (Thames & Hudson, 1971).

To save space in the chart, the names of countries are not given, but will be found in the Index. Thus, at AD 1010–1029 will be found the entry "Mtskheta Cathedral"; in the Index, Mtskheta is identified as being in Georgia (U.S.S.R.). When a building is named in *italics*, it has been destroyed, but enough is known about it to prove its importance. Buildings in the British Isles are in **bold** type.

Date	World Events	Buildings
BC		
753	Rome founded	
740–706		Khorsabad: Palace of Sargon II
705–681		Nineveh: Palace of Sennacherib
c. 680	Coins first issued (in Lydia)	
668–626	Ashurbanipal king of Assyria	
c. 650		Nineveh Palace Library
594	Solon's Laws for Athens	
c. 563	Buddha born	
c. 560		Ephesus: *Temple of Artemis*
551	Confucius born	
518–460		Persepolis: Palace of Darius
c. 510		Paestum: Temple of Demeter
490	Battle of Marathon	
483	Death of Buddha	
480	Battles of Thermopylae and Salamis	
478	Death of Confucius	
c. 460		Paestum: Temple of Poseidon
		Olympia: Temple of Zeus
c. 450–425		Bassae: Temple of Apollo
449–444		Athens: Theseion
447–432		Athens: Parthenon
437–432		Athens: Propylaea
430	Great Plague of Egypt and Greece	
421–405		Athens: Erechtheion
404	Athens conquered by Sparta	
c. 400		China: Great Wall begun
399	Death of Socrates	
356	Alexander the Great born	
355–350		Halicarnassus (Bodrum): Mausoleum
c. 355–330		Ephesus: *Temple of Artemis*
c. 350		Epidauros: Theatre
c. 330		Athens: Theatre of Dionysos
323	Death of Alexander	
313–		Miletus: Temple of Apollo
218	Hannibal crosses the Alps	
174–132		Athens: Olympieion
146	Greece conquered by Rome; Carthage destroyed	
109		Rome: Pons Mulvius Bridge
55	Julius Caesar invades Britain	
c. 48		Athens: Tower of the Winds
44	Caesar murdered	
31	Battle of Actium	
27–AD14	Augustus, Emperor	
16		Nimes: Maison Carrée (Temple)

Date	World Events	Buildings
BC 7	Jesus of Nazareth born	
AD		
c. 10		Segovia: Aqueduct
c. 14		Nimes: Pont du Gard (Aqueduct)
14–20		Rimini: Bridge of Augustus
43	Claudius invades Britain	
c. 50		Orange: Theatre
70	Jerusalem destroyed	
70–82		Rome: Colosseum
71	York founded	
79	Vesuvius erupts: Pompeii destroyed	
80–100		**Caerleon**: Amphitheatre
98–112		Rome: Trajan's Basilica
105–116		Alcantara: Roman Bridge
113		Rome: Trajan's Column
117–138	Hadrian, Emperor	
120–124		Rome: Pantheon
122–126		**Britain**: Hadrian's Wall
135		Rome: Mausoleum of Hadrian
140–142		**Antonine Wall** (Forth to Clyde)
161–180	Marcus Aurelius, Emperor	
174		Rome: Column of Marcus Aurelius
205–208		**Hadrian's Wall rebuilt**
211–217		Rome: Baths of Caracalla
284–305	Diocletian, Emperor	
300		Spalato (Split): Palace and Temple
c. 300		Trier: Porta Nigra (Gateway)
c. 300–305		**York**: Multangular Tower
302		Rome: Baths of Diocletian
306–337	Constantine the Great, Emperor	
310–313		Rome: Basilica of Constantine
313	Christianity made legal	
323–330		Rome: *Old St. Peter's*
324–326		Rome: Church of S. Costanza
327–335		Jerusalem: Church of Anastasis
330	Byzantium (Constantinople) made capital	
361–363	Julian reinstates paganism	
368		Constantinople: Aqueduct
392	Edict of Theodosius (pagan temples closed)	
395	Roman Empire divided	
c. 397		**Whithorn**: *St. Ninian's church*

Date	World Events	Buildings
410	Rome sacked	
413–447		Constantinople: Land Walls
449	Anglo-Saxons begin conquest of Britain	
493–525		Ravenna: S. Apollinare Nuovo
495		Salonica: S. Sophia
512–513		Bosra Cathedral
523		Mt. Sung: Sung-yueh Pagoda
526–547		Ravenna: S. Vitale
527–565	Justinian I, Eastern Emperor	
529	Athens University closed	
		Monte Cassino monastery
530–550		Bethlehem: Church of the Nativity
532–537		Constantinople: S. Sophia
534–539		Ravenna: S. Apollinare in Classe
c. 550?		Ctesiphon: Hall of Chosroes I
558–563		Constantinople: S. Sophia restored
563	St. Columba lands at Iona	
596	Augustine's mission to Britain	
c. 605		China: Imperial Canal begun
605–616		Chao-hsien (Hopei): Great Bridge
618		Vagharshapat: S. Hrip'sime
618–650		Vagharshapat: Etchmiadzin Cathedral
c. 630?		**York**: Anglian Tower
630–640		Mren Cathedral
632	Death of Mohammed	
635–643	Caliph Omar conquers Near East	
644–652		Zvart'nots' church
c. 668		T'alish Cathedral
c. 670		**Brixworth Church**
673–678		**Hexham Church**
674		**Monkwearmouth** monastery
688–691		Jerusalem: Dome of the Rock
c. 690–783		T'alinn Cathedral
701–705		Sian: Wild Goose Pagoda
705–715		Damascus: Great Mosque
711–713	Arabs conquer Spain	
c. 728		Qasr al-Hair: Palace
744–750		Mshatta: Palace
750–786		Damghan: Tarik-khana Mosque
755	Caliphate of Cordova founded	
775–780		Ukhaidir: Palace
784		**Offa's Dyke** made
785–796		Cordova: Great Mosque

Date	World Events	Buildings
786–809	Harun al-Rashid, Caliph of Bagdad	
792–805		Aachen Cathedral
793–794	Kyoto founded	
800	Charlemagne crowned Emperor	
c. 800		Barabudur: Sanctuary
802–839	Egbert, first king of the English	
836–862		Qairawan: Great Mosque
842–850		Naranco: Palace Hall (S. Maria)
847–862		Samarra: Great Mosque
857		Mt. Wutai: Fu-kuang Temple
860		Fez University founded
860–900		Angkor founded
871–899	Alfred the Great, king of England	
876–879		Cairo: Mosque of Ibn Tulun
878	Danes defeated; Treaty of Wedmore	
910		Cluny Abbey founded
911	Duchy of Normandy established	
912–961	Abd ar–Rahman III, Caliph of Cordova	
915–921		Aght'amar: Holy Cross Church
936–961		Medina az–Zahra: Palace
958–966		Oshki Church
961–990		Cordova: Great Mosque extended
970–972		Cairo: Al–Azhar Mosque
c. 975		**Bradford on Avon:** St. Lawrence
984		Chi–hsien (Hopei): Tu-lo Temple
986–1029		Marmashen Cathedral
988	Cairo: Al-Azhar University	
989–1001		Ani Cathedral
990–1013		Cairo: Mosque of al–Hakim
1000	Leif Ericsson discovers America	
c. 1000		Tanjore: Great Temple
		Earls Barton: Church Tower
		Bhuvanesvar: Lingaraj Temple
		Khajuraho: Kandarya Mahadeo Temple
1000–1033		Hildesheim: S. Michael
1003–		Kutais Cathedral
1005–1049		Rheims: S. Rémi
1006–1007		Gunbad-i-Kabus: Monument
1008		Torcello Cathedral
1010–1029		Mtskheta Cathedral
1015–1037		Kiev: S. Sophia Cathedral
1016–1035	Canute, king of England	
1016–1047		Trier Cathedral
c. 1020–1032		Ripoll: S. Maria

Date	World Events	Buildings
1030–1061		Speyer Cathedral
1037–1066		Jumièges Abbey
1040–1050		Goslar: Imperial Hall
1040–1057	Macbeth, king of Scotland	
1042–1085		Venice: S. Mark
1042–1066	Edward the Confessor, king of England	
1045–1052		Novgorod: S. Sophia Cathedral
c. 1050		K'ai–feng (Honan): Iron-coloured Pagoda
1050–1065		**Westminster Abbey** (Norman)
c. 1050–1130		Conques: Ste. Foi
1056		Ying-hsien: Fu-kung-ssu Pagoda
1058–1093	Malcolm, king of Scotland	
c. 1060–1115		St. Savin-sur-Gartempe Abbey
1062–1140		Caen: Abbaye-aux-Dames
1063–1092		Pisa Cathedral
1065	Seljuk Turks invade Asia Minor	
		Diyarbakir Bridge
1066	Battle of Hastings	
1066–1087	William the Conqueror, king of England	
1066–1086		Caen: Abbaye–aux–Hommes
1071	Turks take Jerusalem; defeat Byzantines	
1072–1092		Isfahan: Great Mosque
1074–1092		**Lincoln Cathedral:** west front
1075–1128		Santiago de Compostella Cathedral
1077–1115		**St. Albans Abbey**
1079–1093		**Winchester Cathedral**
1079–1145		**Hereford Cathedral**
1080–1096		Toulouse: S. Sernin
1081–1130		**Bury St. Edmunds Abbey**
1083–1189		**Ely Cathedral**
1084–1090		Pagan: Ananda Temple
1084–1092		**Worcester Cathedral:** crypt
1085–1137		Mainz Cathedral
1086	Domesday Survey	
1087–1092		Cairo: Walls and Gates
1088–1128		Milan: S. Ambrogio
1088–1091		Ávila: City Walls
1089–1100		**Gloucester Cathedral**
1089–1131		Cluny Abbey rebuilt
1091	Chinese Board of Works issues *Methods of Building Construction* (printed 1103)	
1093–1133		**Durham Cathedral**

Date	World Events	Buildings
1093–1156		Maria Laach Abbey
1096	Valencia taken by El Cid	
1096–1099	First Crusade	
1096–1145		**Norwich Cathedral**
1097–1099		**Westminster Hall**
1099	Crusaders take Jerusalem	
1101–1119		Fontevrault Abbey
c. 1104–1132		Vézelay: S. Madeleine
c. 1105–		Ángoulême Cathedral
1106–		Gelati Cathedral
c. 1108–1120		**Winchester Cathedral:** Tower
1109		Bologna: Torre Asinelli
1110–1200		Tournai Cathedral
1113–1150	Suryavarman II, king of Khmer	
c. 1115–1145		Angkor Wat
1117–1128		Diyarbakir: Great Mosque rebuilt
1117–1175		**Peterborough Cathedral**
1118		**Jedburgh Abbey founded**
1120–1150		Lamp'un: Wat Kukut
1120–1160		Périgueux: S. Front
c. 1120–1132		Autun Cathedral
1125		Cairo: Al–Aqmar Mosque
c. 1126		Bitlis: Great Mosque
1128		**Kelso Abbey** founded
1128–		**Holyrood Abbey**
1129–		Siirt: Great Mosque
1130		**Neath Abbey** founded
1131–1200		Cefalù Cathedral
1132–1140		Palermo: Palace Chapel
1133–		**Exeter Cathedral:** Towers
1135–1140		Kayseri: Great Mosque
1135–1143		Fez: Qarawiyin (Great) Mosque
1135–1168		Sens Cathedral
c. 1135–1210		**Fountains Abbey**
1136–		**St. Cross Hospital**
		Melrose Abbey
1137–		**Kirkwall Cathedral**
1137–1144		St. Denis Abbey: new works
1139–1147		Fontenay Abbey
1140–1149		Jerusalem: Church of Holy Sepulchre
1144	Seljuks reconquer Edessa	
1146–1147		Silvan: Batman Su Bridge
1147	Lisbon freed from the Moors	
1150		**Margam Abbey** founded
		Dryburgh Abbey founded
1152–1200		Salamanca Old Cathedral
1153–		Pisa Baptistery

Date	World Events	Buildings
1154–1189	Henry II, king of England	
1156–1220		Konya: Alaüddin Mosque
c. 1160–1211		Ávila Cathedral
1162–1182		Konya: Iplikçi Mosque
1163–		Paris: Notre–Dame Cathedral
1166–		Poitiers Cathedral
c. 1166–1188		Ciudad Rodrigo Cathedral
1168–1211		Santiago de Compostella: Portico
1170	Thomas Becket murdered	
c. 1170		**Durham Cathedral:** Galilee
c. 1171–1289		Tarragona Cathedral
1172–		**Dublin:** Christ Church Cathedral
1174–		Pisa: Campanile (Leaning Tower)
1174–1189		Monreale Cathedral
1175		**Arbroath Abbey founded**
1175–		Urgel Cathedral
1175–1184		**Canterbury Cathedral** Choir
1177–1185		Avignon: St. Benezet Bridge
c. 1177		Konya: *Royal Palace*
1179–		Erzerum: Great Mosque
1180–1203		Burgos: Las Huelgas monastery
c. 1180–		**Wells Cathedral**
1181–1219	Jayavarman VII, king of Khmer	
		Angkor Thom city
1184–1198		Seville: Giralda Tower (Minaret)
1185–1189		Vladimir: Cathedral of Dormition
1187	Saladin takes Jerusalem	
1189–1199		Rabat: Great Mosque
1192–1225		Bourges Cathedral
1192–		**Lincoln Cathedral**
1193–1210		Delhi: Kutub Mosque
c. 1200		Angkor Thom: Bayon Temple
1200–1204		Kiziltepe: Great Mosque
1203–1278		Lérida: Old Cathedral
1204	Franks take Constantinople	
	France takes Normandy	
1206	Jinghiz Khan, Mongol Emperor	
1208	Palencia University founded	
1209–1212		Aleppo: Citadel
1210–		**Kilkenny Cathedral**
1211–		Rheims Cathedral
1215	Magna Carta granted	
c. 1215–1300		Roskilde Cathedral
1217–1254		Le Mans Cathedral
1218	Invasion by Jinghiz Khan	
c. 1220	Salamanca University founded	
1220–		Amiens Cathedral
1220–1266		**Salisbury Cathedral**

Date	World Events	Buildings
c. 1220–1250		Coutances Cathedral
1222–		**Winchester Castle:** Hall
1222–1260		Burgos Cathedral
1224–1270		**Elgin Cathedral**
c. 1225–1231		Kayseri: Agzikara Inn
c. 1225–1250		**York Minster:** Transepts
1225–		**Dublin:** St. Patrick's Cathedral
1226–1228		Alanya: Red Tower and Shipyard
1227–		Toledo Cathedral
1228–1229		Divrigi: Great Mosque, Hospital
1228–1253		Assisi: Church of St. Francis
1229	Emperor Frederick II occupies Jerusalem	
1231–1281		St. Denis Abbey: Nave
1232–1300		El Burgo de Osma Cathedral
1233–1258		**Glasgow Cathedral**
1238–1264		Konaraka: Black Pagoda Temple
1239–1250		**Ely Cathedral:** Presbytery
1240–1300		**Dunblane Cathedral**
1241	Mongols overrun Eastern Europe	
1243–1248		Paris: Sainte Chapelle
1245–		**Westminster Abbey** rebuilt
1247–1272		Beauvais Cathedral
1248–		Cologne Cathedral
1250		Tokat Bridge
1253		Erzerum: Hatuniye Medrese
1255–1303		León Cathedral
1256–1280		**Lincoln Cathedral:** Angel Choir
1257–1283		Marburg: S. Elizabeth
1258		Konya: Ince Minare Medrese
c. 1260–1275		The Hague: Ridderzaal
1261	Byzantines recover Constantinople	
1262–1325		Clermont-Ferrand Cathedral
1262–1356		Valencia Cathedral
1263–1266		Troyes: S. Urbain
1264–		**Oxford:** Merton College
1267–1269		Cairo: Mosque of Baibars I
1268		Sonmathpur (Mysore): Temple
1270–1274	Crusade by Edward I	
1271		Peking: White Pagoda
1271		Sivas: Çifte Minareli Medrese
1271–1272		Sivas: Gök Medrese
1272–		Narbonne Cathedral
1272–1307	Edward I, king of England	
c. 1273–1315		Uppsala Cathedral
1274		Pagan: Mingalazedi Stupa
1276–1439		Strassburg Cathedral
1282–		Albi Cathedral

Date	World Events	Buildings
1284–1293		Cairo: Madrasa of Qalaun
1288–		**Exeter Cathedral**
1291–1294		**Eleanor Crosses**
1291–1321		**York Minster:** Nave
1292–1348		**Westminster:** St. Stephen's Chapel
1293	Christian missionaries reach China	
1295		Konya: Tomb of Rumi
c. 1295		Pagan: Mahabodhi Temple
1298–1329		Barcelona Cathedral
c. 1300–1384		Marienwerder Cathedral
1305		Ermenak Bridge
1306		Padua: Palazzo della Ragione
1306–1406		Palma de Mallorca Cathedral
1307–1311		**Lincoln Cathedral:** Central Tower
1307–1313		Sultanieh: Mausoleum of Uljaitu
1308	Turks enter Europe Coimbra University founded	
1308–1380		Cahors: Valentré Bridge
1309		Amasya: Yildiz Hatun Hospital
c. 1310–1320		Tabriz: Mosque of Ali Shah
1312–1386		Gerona Cathedral
1313	Invention of Gunpowder Great Famine in Europe	
1314–1315		
1319–1536		Rouen: Abbey of St. Ouen
1320–1364		Cracow Cathedral
1322–1346		**Ely Cathedral:** Octagon
1323		Foochow: Bridge of 10,000 Ages
1323–1325		Fez: Attarine Madrasa
1324	Aztecs found Mexico City	
1326	Turks take Bursa	
1327–1377	Edward III, king of England	
1331–1376		Soest: Wiesenkirche
1332–1349		**London:** *Old St. Paul's Chapter House*
1334–1354		Granada: Alhambra
1338	Edward III visits Rhineland	
1343–1404		Venice: Doge's Palace
1343–1502		Danzig: S. Mary
1344–1352		Avignon: Palace of the Popes
1344–		Prague Cathedral
1347–1355		**Chester:** Dee Bridge
1348	Order of the Garter founded	
1349–		Kerman: Great Mosque
1349	Black Death (1st Plague)	
1350–1355		Fez: Bou Inaniya Madrasa
1350–1356		**Windsor Castle:** Dean's Cloister

Date	World Events	Buildings
1352–1411		Antwerp Cathedral
1356–1363		Cairo: Mosque of Sultan Hassan
1359–1370		Barcelona: Tinell (Royal Hall)
1359–		Vienna Cathedral: Nave
c. 1360–		Cracow: S. Mary
1361	The 2nd Plague	
	Turks take Adrianople (Edirne)	
1364–1366		Seville: Alcazar Palace
1366–1376		Manisa: Great Mosque
1366–1385		Bursa: Hudavendigar Mosque
1368	Mongols overthrown in China	
1369	The 3rd Plague	
1374–1375		Selçuk: Isa Bey Mosque
1375–		**Westminster Abbey:** Nave
1377–1399	Richard II, king of England	
1377–1405		**Canterbury Cathedral:** Nave
1377–		**Granada:** Alhambra Court of Lions
1377–1492		Ulm Cathedral
1378		Iznik: Green Mosque
1380–1386		**Oxford:** New College
1380–1480		Kassa: S. Elizabeth
1387–1397		**Rochester:** *Old Bridge*
1387–1434		Batalha Monastery
1387–		Milan Cathedral
1387–1402		**Winchester College**
1390–1395		Bursa: Yildirim Mosque
1390–1405		Kesh: Timur's Palace
1391–1395		Cracow: Cloth Hall
1393–1468		Brunswick: Old Town Hall
1394–1400		**Westminster Hall** rebuilt
1394–1450		**Winchester Cathedral** Nave
1396	Turks defeat Christians at Nicopolis	
1396–1400		Bursa: Great Mosque
1397		Kinkakuji: Golden Pavilion
1398	Timur takes Delhi	
c. 1401–1448		**Perth:** St. John's Choir
1402	Korea: Printing from movable type	
1402–1498		Seville Cathedral
1403–1414		Edirne: Old Mosque
1405		Samarkand: Tomb of Timur
1409		Nigde: Ak Medrese
1409–1424		(Peking): Ming Tombs
1411–1430		**London:** Guildhall
1412	St. Andrew's University founded	
1419–1424		Bursa: Green Mosque
1419–1522		sHertogenbosch Cathedral

Date	World Events	Buildings
1420–		Peking: Temple of Heaven
1420	Treaty of Troyes	
1420–1434		Florence Cathedral: Dome
1421–1425		**Catterick Bridge**
1421–1424		Florence: Foundling Hospital
1424–1442		**Aberdeen Cathedral:** Nave
1430–1444		Kolozsvár: S. Michael
1431	Caen University founded	
1433–		Peking: City Walls
1437–		**Barnstaple Bridge**
1437–1447		Edirne: Üç Şerefeli Mosque
1438–1443		**Oxford:** All Souls College
1438–1471	Pachacuti, Emperor of the Incas	
1440	European reinvention of Printing	
1441–1460		**Eton College**
1441–		**Herstmonceux Castle**
1441–1447		Cologne: Gürzenich (Dance Hall)
1443–1515		**Cambridge:** King's College Chapel
1444–1460		Florence: Palazzo Riccardi
1446–		**Roslin Chapel**
c. 1450–1480		Cuzco: Sacshuaman fortress
1451	Glasgow University founded	
1452		Istanbul: Rumeli Hisar
1453	Turks take Constantinople	
1453–1455	First printed Bible	
1455–1485	Wars of the Roses	
1458–1465		Florence: Pitti Palace
1463–1471		Istanbul: *Mohammed II Mosque*
1465–		Tabriz: Blue Mosque
1468–1488		Munich: Frauenkirche
c. 1470		Stockholm: Great Church
1472		Istanbul: Çinili Kiosk
1473		Peking: Ta–chen–chueh Temple
1474–1475		Cairo: Tomb and Mosque of Qaitbay
1474–1490		**Oxford:** Magdalen College
1475–1479		Moscow: Dormition Cathedral
1475–1480		**Eltham Palace:** Hall
1475–1528		**Windsor:** St. George's Chapel
1476	Caxton's first printing press	
1480–		**Oxburgh Hall**
1480–1492		Guadalajara Palace
1482–1498		Valencia Exchange
1484–1488		Edirne: Beyazit Mosque
1485	Battle of Bosworth	
	L. B. Alberti: *De l'Architettura*	

Date	World Events	Buildings
1486–1498		Rome: Palazzo della Cancelleria
1486	Vitruvius first printed (Rome)	
–1487		Mexico City: Great Temple
1488–1495		Manisa: Hatuniye Mosque
1489–1539		Florence: Palazzo Strozzi
1490–		**Oxford:** Magdalen Tower
1492	Columbus discovers America Spaniards conquer Granada	
1492–1497		Cracow University
1492–1513		Thomar: Convent
1493–1503		Prague: Vladislav Hall
1493–1505		**Canterbury Cathedral:** Central Tower
1496–1508		**Peterborough Cathedral:** Eastern Chapels
1497	Vasco da Gama rounds Cape	
1498–1548		Plasencia Cathedral
1499–1503		**Edinburgh:** Old Holyrood Palace
1499–1526		Rouen: Palace of Justice
1500		Hoşap Bridge
1500–1506		**Aberdeen:** King's College Chapel
1500–1522		Belem: Jeronimos
1501–1506		Istanbul: Beyazit Mosque
1501–1539		**Bath Abbey**
1502–1522		**Ripon Cathedral:** Nave
1503–1519		**Westminster:** Henry VII's Chapel
1505	First regular mail (Vienna–Brussels)	
1505–1525		**Wrexham Church:** Tower
1506–1626		Rome: St. Peter's
1508–1640		Blois: Chateau
1512–1514		Salamanca: Casa de las Conchas
1512–1588		Salamanca: New Cathedral
1515–1536		**Hampton Court Palace**
1515–1576		Chenonceaux: Chateau
1517	Turks conquer Syria and Egypt	
1518–1520		Diyarbakir: Fatih Pasha Mosque
1518–1527		Azay–le–Rideau: Chateau
1519–1547		Chambord: Chateau
1519–1556	Charles V, Emperor	
c. 1520		Konya: Selimiye Mosque
c. 1520–1522		Istanbul: Sultan Selim Mosque
1520–1527		**Aberdeen:** Bridge of Dee
1520–1532		**Winchester Cathedral:** Presbytery
1521	Turks take Belgrade	

Date	World Events	Buildings
1521	Cesariano's edition of Vitruvius	
1521–1534		Florence: Medici Chapel
1523–1527		**Sutton Place**
1525–1529		**Oxford:** Christ Church (Cardinal College)
1525–1538		**Hengrave Hall**
1525–1591		Segovia Cathedral
1526	India conquered by Babur	
1528–1540		Fontainebleau Palace
1528–1563		Granada Cathedral
1528–1632		Malaga Cathedral
1530–1546		Rome: Palazzo Farnese
1531–1612		Heidelberg Castle
1532		Kolomenskoe: Church of Ascension
1533	Henry VIII's Divorce	
1536–1540	Dissolution of English monasteries	
1536–1545		Aleppo: Hüsrev Pasha Mosque
1537–1553		Alcalá de Henares University
1539–		**Stirling Palace**
1540–1579		Jaén Cathedral
1542–1579		Toledo: Tavera Hospital
1543–1548		Istanbul: Şehzade Mosque
1545	Padua: first Botanic Garden founded	
1545–1614		Vicenza: Basilica
1546–		Paris: Louvre
1546–1602		**Cambridge:** Trinity College
1547–1552		**London:** *Old Somerset House*
1550–1557		Istanbul: Suleymaniye Mosque
1555–1560		Moscow: Cathedral of S. Basil
1556		Istanbul: Haseki Baths
1559–1584		The Escorial
1561–1566		Antwerp: Town Hall
1562–1565		Istanbul: Mihrimah Mosque
1562–1572		**London:** Middle Temple Hall
1563–		(Istanbul): Büyükçekmece Bridge
1563	John Shute, *The First and Chief Groundes of Architecture in England*	
1563–1667		Mexico Cathedral
1565		Old Delhi: Tomb of Humayun
1565–1610		Venice: S. Giorgio Maggiore
1567	Philibert de l'Orme: *L'Architecture*	
1567–1580		**Longleat House**
1568–1584		Rome: Gesu Church
1569	Mercator's Map of the World	
1569–1575		Edirne: Selimiye Mosque
1569–1585	Andrea Palladio: *dell' Architettura*	Fatehpur-Sikri: city

Date	World Events	Buildings
1570–1572		Istanbul: Sokollu Mehmet Pasha Mosque
1570–1575		**Kirby Hall**
1571	Turks take Cyprus and Tunis Battle of Lepanto	
1571–1576		Bijapur: Great Mosque
1577–1578		Istanbul: Azapkapi Mosque
1577–1583		Istanbul: Eski Valide Mosque
1577–1587		**Burghley House**
1580		Istanbul: Kiliç Ali Pasha Mosque
1580–1599		**Montacute House**
1583–1586		Manisa: Muradiye Mosque
1590–1597		**Hardwick Hall**
1596	Galileo invents Thermometer	
1597–1663		Istanbul: New Mosque
1603–1615		Istanbul: Davut Pasha Palace
1603–1616		**Audley End**
1605–1612		**Bramshill House**
1607–1611		**Hatfield House**
1607–1612		**Charlton House**
1609–1616		Istanbul: Sultan Ahmet Mosque
1610–1613		**Oxford:** Wadham College
1613–1636		**Oxford:** Bodleian Library
1614	Napier invents Logarithms	
1614–1628		Salzburg Cathedral
1615–1624		Paris: Luxembourg Palace
1616–1635		**Greenwich:** Queen's House
1619–1622		**Whitehall:** Banqueting House
1626–		**Blickling Hall**
1628–1638		Rome: Palazzo Barberini
1630–1653		Agra: Taj Mahal
1631–1682		Venice: S. Maria della Salute
1632	Oxford Botanic Garden founded	
1633–1635		The Hague: Mauritshuis
1636	Harvard College founded	
1636–1659		Bijapur: Gol Gombaz
1638–1639		Istanbul: Bagdad Pavilion
1642–1646	Civil War in England	
1643–1715	Louis XIV, king of France	
1645–1647		Peking: Wu Men Gate and Forbidden City Halls
1647–1649		**Wilton House**
1648–1665		Amsterdam: Royal Palace
1649–1654		Yaroslavl: S. John Chrysostom
1649–1656		The Hague: The New Church
1652		Peking: White Dagoba
1660		Istanbul: Egyptian Bazaar
1660–1685	Charles II, king of Great Britain	

Date	World Events	Buildings
1661–1756		Versailles Palace
1663–		**Greenwich Hospital**
1666	Great Fire of London	
1667–1756		Venice: Palazzo Rezzonico
1669	Turks take Crete	
1672–1679		**London:** St. Stephen Walbrook
1675–1706		Paris: Invalides Hospital
1675–1710		**London:** St. Paul's Cathedral
1677–1766		Saragossa: El Pilar Cathedral
1678	Bunyan: *Pilgrim's Progress*	
1678–1694		Wilanow Palace
1679–		Turin: Palazzo Carignano
1680	Purcell: *Dido and Aeneas*	
	London Penny Post	
1681	French Canal du Midi opened	
1682–1692		**Chelsea Hospital**
1688	English Revolution	
1691–1699		Pskov: Trinity Cathedral
1692		Warsaw: Krasinski Palace
1694	Bank of England established	
1695–1851	Window Tax	
1698–		Paris: Place Vendome
1698–1706		Berlin Palace
1699	Australia first explored by Dampier	
1699–1726		**Castle Howard**
1702–1736		Melk: Monastery
1705–1720		**Blenheim Palace**
1709–1725		**Birmingham:** St. Philip (Cathedral)
1709–1738		**Oxford:** Queen's College
1710–1719		Würzburg: The Neumünster
1711–1722		Dresden: The Zwinger
1713–1716		Vienna: Belvedere Palace
1714–1725		St. Petersburg: SS. Peter and Paul Cathedral
1715–		Valladolid University
1719–1739		La Granja Palace
1720–1744		Würzburg Residency
1721–1724		Vienna: The Upper Belvedere
1722	J. S. Bach: *Wohltemperiertes Klavier*	
1722–1726		**London:** St. Martin in the Fields
1722–1730		**Cambridge:** Senate House
1722–1832		Cadiz Cathedral
1725–		Chiswick House
1727–1747		Dresden: Frauenkirche
1727–1764		Granada: Charterhouse
1728		Istanbul: Ahmet III Fountain
1734–		**Holkham Hall**

Date	World Events	Buildings
1735–1748		**Bath:** Prior Park
1737–1749		**Oxford:** Radcliffe Library
1737–1754		Murcia Cathedral: West front
1738–1749		Santiago de Compostella
		Cathedral: West front
1742	Handel: *Messiah*	
	B. & T. Langley: *Ancient* (Gothic)	
	Architecture Restored and Improved	
1743–1772		Vierzehnheiligen: Church
1745–1747		Potsdam: Sanssouci Palace
1746–1845	Excise Duty on Glass	
1747–1776		**Twickenham:** Strawberry Hill
1748–1755		Istanbul: Nuruosmaniye Mosque
1749	J. S. Bach: *Art of Fugue*	
1749–1756		Tsarskoe Selo: Great Palace
1750–1758		**Whitehall:** The Horse Guards
1751–1756		Karlsruhe: Schloss
1752–1755		**Pontypridd Bridge**
1754–		**Bath:** The Circus
1754–1762		St. Petersburg: Winter Palace
1755	Samuel Johnson: *Dictionary*	
1757	William Chambers: *Design of*	
	Chinese Buildings	
1757–1759		**Old Eddystone Lighthouse**
1757–1770		**Kedleston Hall**
1757–1790		Paris: Panthéon
(1758)–1766	George Stubbs: *Anatomy of the Horse*	
1759–1763		Istanbul: Laleli Mosque
1759–1771		**Harewood House**
1760–1820	George III, king of Great Britain	
1762–1768		Versailles: Petit Trianon
1762–1816	*The Antiquities of Athens* (4 volumes)	
1764	Robert Adam: *Ruins . . . at Spalatro*	
1767–1775		**Bath:** Royal Crescent
1767–1795		Warsaw: Lazienki Palace
1771–1779		**Stowe House**
1776–1786		**London:** Somerset House
1776–1802		**Dublin:** The Four Courts
1777	Sheridan: *The School for Scandal*	
1777–1781		**Tetbury Church**
1777–1790		**Culzean Castle**
1778		**Coalbrookdale:** Iron Bridge
1780–1803		Vich Cathedral
1781–1791		**Dublin:** Custom House
1782–1785		St. Petersburg: The Hermitage
1784–1789		Paris: Barrière de la Villette
1784–1850	Tax on Bricks	
1785	Mozart: *Marriage of Figaro*	

Date	World Events	Buildings
1787	Mozart: *Don Giovanni*	
1788–1833		**London:** Bank of England
1789–1793		Berlin: Brandenburg Gate
1789–1795	French Revolution	
1789–1798		Richmond (Va): State Capitol
1791	Mozart: *The Magic Flute*	
1792–1829		Washington White House
1792–1867		Washington (DC) The Capitol
1796–1807		**Fonthill** *"Abbey"*
1797–1804		**Knottingley:** Ferry Bridge
1799	Haydn: *The Creation*	
1805	Battle of Trafalgar	
1806–1842		Paris: The Madeleine
1810–1817		**London:** *Old Waterloo Bridge*
1812	Invasion of Russia by Napoleon	
1813	Jane Austen: *Pride and Prejudice*	
1813–1817		**London:** Custom House
1815	Battle of Waterloo	
1815–1821		**Brighton:** Royal Pavilion
1818	Atlantic first crossed by steam	
1819–1826		**Menai Suspension Bridge**
1820–1824		**Chelsea:** St. Luke
1823–1847		**London:** The British Museum
1824–1826		**Conway Suspension Bridge**
1824–1828		Berlin: Altes Museum
1825	First public railway opened	
1827–1829		**London:** University College
1827–1832		**Chester:** Grosvenor Bridge
1833		Warsaw: Grand Theatre
1833–1836		**Edinburgh:** Royal Scottish Institution
1834–1838		**London:** National Gallery
1834–1840		**Norwich:** Yarn Mill
1836–1840		**Chatsworth:** *Conservatory*
1837–1901	Victoria, Queen of Great Britain	
1837–1847		**Cambridge:** Fitzwilliam Museum
1838–1840		**London:** Reform Club
1840–1860		**Westminster:** Houses of Parliament
1842–1854		**Liverpool:** St. George's Hall
1845–1850		**Menai Strait:** Britannia Bridge
1845–1857		**Kew:** The Palm House
1849–1859		**London:** All Saints, Margaret Street
1850–1851		**London:** *Crystal Palace*
1850–1854		**Edinburgh:** National Gallery of Scotland

Date	World Events	Buildings
1851–1852		**London:** Kings Cross Station
1855	Electric bulb invented	
1855–1859		**Oxford:** University Museum
1857	First Atlantic cable completed	
1859–1860		**Bexley Heath:** The Red House
1860–1875		**London:** Foreign Office
1861–1865	American Civil War	
1865–1874		**London:** Midland Grand Hotel
1868–1877		**Manchester:** Town Hall
1869	First transcontinental (USA) railway opened	
1870	Franco-Prussian War	
1870–1880		(**London**): Kilburn, St. Augustine
1873–1876		**Oxford:** Keble College Chapel
1874	International Postal Union founded	
1874–1882		**London:** Royal Courts of Justice
1880–1884		Garabit Viaduct
1880–1910		**Truro Cathedral**
1882–1890		**Forth Bridge**
1883–		Barcelona: Church of Sagrada Familia
1885–1887		Chicago: Marshall Field Warehouse
1885–1889		Barcelona: Güell Palace
1887–1889		Paris: Eiffel Tower
1887–1893		Boston (USA): Public Library
1891–1904	Trans-Siberian Railway built	
1893–1902		Copenhagen: Town Hall
1895–1903		**Westminster:** Roman Catholic Cathedral
1897–1909		**Glasgow:** School of Art
1898	Spanish–American War	
1899–1902	Boer War in South Africa	
1903–		**Liverpool Cathedral**
1904–1905	Russo-Japanese War	
1904–1914		Helsinki: Railway Station
1905–1906		Tavanasa: Rhine Bridge
1905–1910		Barcelona: Casa Milá
1906		**Roker:** St. Andrew's Church
1909		Berlin: AEG Turbine Factory
1910–1913		Pretoria: Union Buildings
1911–1923		Stockholm: Town Hall
1911–1927		Stuttgart: Railway Station
1913–1930		New Delhi: Government Buildings
1914–1918	World War I	
1919	Atlantic first crossed by air	

Date	World Events	Buildings
1920	First wireless broadcasting	
1921–1926		Copenhagen: Grundtvigs Church
1922–1926		(Paris) Le Raincy: Notre Dame
1923		Hamburg: Chilehaus
1923–1926		**Westminster:** Horticultural Hall
1924–1932		Sydney: Harbour Bridge
1928–1932		Hilversum: Town Hall
1929–1930		Salginatobel Bridge
1930–1934		**Swansea:** City Hall
1932–1934		**London:** R.I.B.A. Building
1932–1938		**Norwich:** City Hall
1933–1937		San Francisco: Golden Gate Bridge
1936		Florence: Railway Station
1937–1941		(Dublin): Collinstown Airport
1938		Orbetello: Aircraft Hanger
1939–1945	World War II	
1948–1950		Turin: Exhibition Hall
1950		Raleigh (N. Carolina): Arena
1950–1951		Rome: Termini Station
1950–1952		New York: Lever House
		Rio de Janeiro: Pedregulho Housing
1956–1957		Rome: Palazzetto dello Sport
1956–1959		New York: Guggenheim Museum
1956–		Brasilia: Federal capital city
		Sydney: Opera House
1957–1958		Johannesburg: Railway Station
1958–1963		(Washington, DC): Dulles Airport
		Sydney: Gladesville Bridge
1958–1964		**Forth Road Bridge**
1959		Rome: Palazzo dello Sport
1959–1964		Tokyo: Shinjuka Station
1961		Tokyo: Metropolitan Festival Hall
1961–1966		**Severn Bridge**
1962–1966		Lisbon: Salazar Bridge
1967		**York:** Theatre Royal extension

Glossary

ABBEY. A monastery ruled by an abbot, with an assistant called a prior (see Priory).

ACROPOLIS. A citadel on top of a hill above an ancient Greek city.

AISLE. A wing separated from the central part of a building by a row of columns or piers.

APSE. A semicircular or polygonal projection from a building, especially around the altar of a church.

ARCADE. A row of arches; usually opposed to Colonnade.

ARCUATED. Arched; used in opposition to Trabeated, of the two main types of construction.

ART NOUVEAU. "New Art"; a style of decoration used between about 1890 and 1910.

ASHLAR. Accurate masonry of squared blocks in regular courses.

BANKER. The bench on which stone is worked.

BAPTISTERY. A building made to contain the font for baptism.

BAROQUE. A fantastic style of movement, away from the static qualities of the Renaissance.

BASE. The foot of a wall, and especially of a column.

BASILICA. A large hall, used in Roman times as an exchange and a law-court.

BAY. A compartment of a building between two columns, buttresses or roof trusses.

BED. The lower and upper surfaces of a worked stone; the natural stratification of stone in a quarry.

BELFRY. Originally a watch tower, but generally used for a bell tower (see also Campanile).

BUTTRESS. A mass of masonry built against a wall to resist Thrust.

BYZANTINE. The style of architecture used in Byzantium (Constantinople, now Istanbul) from AD 330 until about 1500.

CAME. A thin strip of lead of H section, used for joining panes or pieces of glass in old windows.

CAMPANILE. A bell tower (Italian).

CANOPY. A projection above a door, statue, etc., often ornamental.

CAPITAL. The crowning part of a column or pier, carrying beams or arches.

CENTRING. Temporary framework to support arches and vaults in course of construction.

CHANCEL. The part of a church for clergy and choir, originally separated by a screen (Latin *cancellus*).

EAST FRONT c. 1331
THOMAS OF CANTERBURY
ST. STEPHEN'S CHAPEL, WESTMINSTER

CHANTRY. An endowment to sing masses on behalf of the souls of the dead; a chapel (in full, Chantry Chapel) for the purpose.

CHAPTER HOUSE. The room at a monastery or cathedral used for meetings of the chapter or governing body.

CINQUEFOIL. A five-leaf form produced by cusps in the head of a window or in a circle.

CLERESTORY. An upper range of windows, usually above the roof of an aisle.

CLOISTER. A courtyard surrounded by a covered walk; in monasteries usually square and placed centrally so as to link all the buildings.

COLONNADE. A row of columns, usually supporting a beam, as opposed to an Arcade.

CORBEL. A projection to support some upper feature, often a roof timber.

CORNICE. The topmost projecting part of a Classical building.

CRYPT. An underground chamber, generally beneath a church.

CUPOLA. A little dome; a turret covered with a small dome.

CUSP. A point projecting from inside the curve of an arch or decorative tracery.

DECORATED. A period of English architecture after the Early English, lasting from about 1250 to 1350. Its main characteristic was the use of bar-tracery in curving forms, at first of circles (Geometrical), later using Ogee curves (Curvilinear).

DOG-TOOTH. An ornament resembling a row of teeth, formed of small pyramids, usually in the hollow of a moulding. It is typical of the Early English period.

DORMER. A window projecting from the slope of a roof.

EARLY ENGLISH. The first period of English Gothic architecture, after the Transition from Norman Romanesque. It lasted from the latter part of the twelfth century until about 1250, when it began to be superseded by Decorated. The sharply pointed Lancet arch is typical of the style.

ELIZABETHAN. The English style of the reign of Elizabeth I, 1558–1603. Basic construction remained Gothic (i.e. late Tudor), but there were many Renaissance features in design.

FLAMBOYANT. A development of the flowing tracery of the later Decorated style, in which the shapes are like flames. Though invented in England about 1320 these forms were mainly used on the continent and in Scotland from about 1400 onwards.

FOIL. Each of the small spaces between Cusps (Latin *folium*, a leaf).

ELY CATHEDRAL
LADY CHAPEL c. 1330

GABLE. The triangular end of a roof; also the whole of the end wall beneath and including this.

GALILEE. Usually a western porch; at Durham Cathedral a chapel added outside the west front.

GEORGIAN. The time of the first four Georges, kings of England, 1714–1830; as a name for an architectural style generally limited to the period before 1810 (see Regency).

GOTHIC. The name given to the style of architecture based on the pointed arch, introduced in the twelfth century and progressing until the sixteenth.

GOTHIC REVIVAL. A style in architecture based on historical romanticism and copying the forms of Gothic. Though preceded by earlier attempts, the style flourished from 1820 to 1880; its last notable work is Liverpool Cathedral, begun 1903.

GREEK REVIVAL. A version of the Renaissance style, copying the forms of Greek rather than Roman work. It was based primarily upon the publication of the first volume of The Antiquities of Athens (by James Stuart and Nicholas Revett) in 1762, and flourished until after 1820.

"HALF-TIMBER". An incorrect term commonly used for timber-framed construction.

HAMMER-BEAM. A beam projecting as a bracket in some kinds of roof trusses.

JACOBEAN. The style in use during the reign of James VI (of Scotland) and I (of England), 1603–1625.

KEEP. The main stone tower of Norman and some later castles.

KEYSTONE. The central stone of an arch. Keystones were not generally used for pointed arches.

LANCET. A tall narrow window with a pointed untraceried head shaped like the surgical instrument.

LANTERN. A tower with windows lighting the church or house below; also an open upper stage (usually polygonal) of a tower.

LINTEL. A horizontal timber or stone set over an opening to carry the weight above.

LODGE. The building or shed used by craftsmen as a shelter for work at the bench or banker.

MANNERISM. A name given to the later Renaissance style in Italy, preceding Baroque (c. 1550–1630).

MEDIAEVAL. Belonging to the Middle Ages, between the fall of Rome (5th century) and the Renaissance (15th century). In architecture often used to include the Romanesque and Gothic periods together (AD 800–1600).

MINARET. The tower from which Muslims are called to prayer.

MOULDINGS. The contours cut on blocks of stone or pieces of timber, giving light and shade to the design.

NAVE. The central part of a church between Aisles; more especially the arm of a church intended for the congregation and opposite to the Chancel.

NORMAN. A form of the Romanesque style, brought from Normandy to England about 1050, and transformed into Gothic in the twelfth century.

OGEE. A compound (S form) curve.

ORDER. (1) One of the five "Orders of Architecture" used by the Greeks and Romans; (2) One of the rings of an arch built up concentrically.

PALLADIAN. A version of Renaissance style named after Andrea Palladio (1518–1580), author of an Italian book on architecture (1570). His style was used in England by Inigo Jones (1573–1652) and revived in the early Georgian period.

PERPENDICULAR. The name given by Thomas Rickman to the last period of English Gothic style, after the Decorated. It began soon after 1330 and continued until the Renaissance, about 1550. Its later phases (from about 1475) are better described as Tudor.

PIER. A vertical mass of masonry, distinguished from a Column or Shaft circular on plan.

PINNACLE. A solid turret on top of a buttress or used as a feature rising from a wall.

PORTICO. An entrance or porch formed with a row of columns.

PRESBYTERY. The part of a church used by the priests, between the choir and the altar.

PRIORY. A monastery governed by a prior and subordinate to an Abbey.

PURLIN. A roof-beam running lengthwise, carried by the trusses or principals and supporting the common rafters.

PUTLOG. A short horizontal timber used to carry the staging of a scaffold.

QUATREFOIL. A four-leaf form (see also Cinquefoil, Foil, Trefoil).

REGENCY. Strictly the period 1810–1820, when the Prince of Wales was Regent for his father George III. As a style of architecture, commonly used for the whole period 1810–1840.

RENAISSANCE. Literally, a rebirth. The style of architecture directly based upon the study of Roman ruins and upon the written work of Vitruvius. It flourished from about 1400 to 1550. The word is more loosely applied to the whole period of modern history from the fifteenth to the twentieth century, as distinct from Classical and Mediaeval times.

REREDOS. A wall or screen behind an altar.

RIB. An arch supporting a vault, or a section of similar mouldings forming a pattern on a vault.

WESTMINSTER PALACE
ST STEPHEN'S CRYPT
c. 1320
MICHAEL OF CANTERBURY

RIDGE. The angle at the apex of a roof. Also used for a long timber beam or ridgepiece under the ridge itself.

ROCOCO. French for "rockwork", originally used in grottoes. Applied to the flowing style of irregular scrolls which succeeded Baroque and was used through the middle of the eighteenth century, especially in France.

ROMANESQUE. Architecture based on Roman models. The term is particularly applied to the style which began in Italy about AD 800 and was superseded by Gothic in the twelfth century.

SANCTUARY. The eastern part of a Chancel, containing the altar.

SARACENIC. The Muslim style of architecture.

SCREEN. A partition, enclosure or trellis dividing the parts of a church or a hall.

SHAFT. A column, between base and capital; a slender column used in Mediaeval architecture; a vertical moulded member of a pier.

SHRINE. A chest for sacred relics.

SPAN. The space between two walls or supports of a beam, arch or roof.

SPIRE. The pointed roof above a tower.

STEEPLE. A tower crowned by a spire; also used of towers generally, some with spires and some without.

STUCCO. A hard plaster used on the outside of buildings to imitate masonry.

THRUST. The outward pressure of an arch, vault or roof against its supports.

TIE-BAR, TIE-BEAM. A bar (of metal) or beam (of wood) fixed so as to restrain Thrust and prevent overturning of walls or supports.

TOOLING. The marking of the surface of masonry by the axe, chisel or other metal tool driven across it.

TRABEATED. Beamed, as opposed to Arcuated.

TRACERY. Patternwork pierced through the head of a window in Saracenic and Gothic architecture; also unpierced imitations on solid surfaces.

TRACING HOUSE. A room or shed used in the Middle Ages for drawing the designs and details of buildings. It was provided with tracing (drawing) boards and often with a floor of plaster on which geometry could be set out to full size.

TRANSEPT. The cross-arm of a church; or one half of this.

TRANSOM. A horizontal crossbar in a window.

TREFOIL. A three-leaf form (see also Cinquefoil, Foil, Quatrefoil).

TRIFORIUM. The space corresponding to the roofs over the aisles of a church, between Arcade and Clerestory, commonly filled with a pierced gallery.

TUDOR. Named from the Tudor dynasty in England (1485–1603), but applied to the late Gothic style from about 1475. It was followed from 1558 by Elizabethan.

TURRET. A small tower.

VAULT. An arched roof of stone or brick; or a roof imitating the form of this.

VOUSSOIR. One of the wedge-shaped blocks of which an arch is built.

CHARTHAM, KENT
EAST WINDOW
? c.1330

Index

Figures in *italics* refer to illustrations. The letter A after names indicates architects and other designers of buildings. Page numbers from 99 to 118 indicate entries in the Date Chart.

Picture Credits

The author and publishers would like to thank the following for permission to reproduce pictures of theirs on the pages indicated: the trustees of the British Museum, 8, 17, 63; Crown Copyright, Royal Commission on Historical Monuments, 10, 12, 23–8, 35–7, 42, 44–5, 46 (top and bottom l.), 54–8, 69, 72–3, 78–81, 82 (top and middle), 83–4, 88, 92, 94; A. F. Kersting, 46 (bottom r.), 67, 82 (bottom), 86; Batsford, 68; Emile Godfrey, 71.